D1281891

BUDDY STALL'S

CRESCENT CITY

By Gaspar J. "Buddy" Stall

Dedicated To

**Aunt Lucy, Uncle Charlie
and my cousins,
Netsy and Gaspar**

**If God made better people,
I have not had the pleasure of
meeting them.**

Acknowledgements

Clyde Morrison, Lane Casteix, Irvin Bergeron, Marietta & Richard Herr, Joe D'Aquin, Judge Dick Garvey, Julie Dawson, as well as the following:

Collin Hamer and the entire staff of the Louisiana Division of the New Orleans Public Library, Pamela Arceneaux and the entire staff of the Historic New Orleans Collection

FOREWORD

There was a time in history, not long ago, when you purchased a bottle of cow's milk, the cream (the tasty part) was in the neck of the bottle at the top, which substantiated the old adage that cream always comes to the top. Today, all milk purchased is homogenized, meaning the cream and milk have been thoroughly mixed.

The author's goal in presenting the historical information in this book is likened to the one-time cream at the top of the bottle. For your convenience, enjoyment and education, large volumes of historical information have been digested and separated so that only the cream is left for you to enjoy.

CONTENTS

CHAPTER ONE

POTPOURRI

INTRODUCTION

Potpourri, as defined in Webster's Dictionary, is a miscellaneous collection. The potpourri in this chapter runs the gamut. It starts out with the city's nicknames and how they were derived. Big and small are covered in "largest baby ever born" and "smallest park". Unique material includes moving of a five-story, ten-million-pound building, men walking across the Mississippi River, and white alligators with green eyes. Opposites include churches and a street named Gallatin but called "hell on earth" by those who came in contact with it. Also included are the city's ten greatest news stories. Like today's news, the majority were not even close to being pleasant events. The chapter does end on a happy note. It is a simple story, with a moral, entitled "Bread". The title may be simple, but I feel confident you will find the moral to be profound.

NEW ORLEANS
ISLE OF ORLEANS-CRESCENT CITY-BIG EASY-
CITY THAT CARE FORGOT

Many cities have nicknames attached to them. One good example is New York. As most everyone knows, it is referred to as the Big Apple.

The City of New Orleans, after not too many years, received its first nickname. The surveyors, after mapping out the area, found that the city was actually surrounded by water. As you can see from the map (marked Isle of Orleans), the city was virtually surrounded by water when founded. To the north of the city is Lake Pontchartrain. The Mississippi River lies to the south, and Lake Borgne to the east. The entire western side of the city was made up of swamps and marshes. Upon learning this startling fact, the city was referred to as the Isle of Orleans.

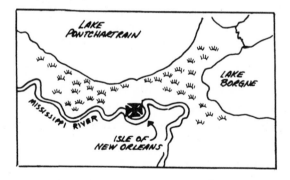

In 1837, the nickname that became associated and used most was born out of a special event. In that year, the first hot air balloon made its way to the city. Its pilot was an experienced balloonist from France. People throughout the area, upon learning of the newfangled flying machine, were drawn to the event like buzzards to a roadkill. Their expectation and excitement were totally fulfilled. As the beautifully colored balloon lifted higher and higher, the roar from the appeased crowd seemed to be focused on the balloon. As it rose, the cheers got louder and louder. When reaching its maximum height, the massive balloon seemed to be just a fraction of its enormous size.

Those who witnessed the first aerial flight by a hot air balloon in New Orleans no doubt had that image burned into their memories for the rest of their lives.

Upon descending and landing, the pilot nonchalantly made reference to the beautiful crescent in the river. A news-

paper correspondent picked up on the new description and made reference to it in writing of the event. Until this day, New Orleans is affectionately called the Crescent City, even though today the largest part of the city is located outside the crescent of the river.

Another more recent name attached to the area is the Big Easy. In 1989, a movie was shot in the area. You, no doubt, have already guessed its title, "The Big Easy".

There is one other name or description of New Orleans. Some natives take offense to it. It is felt that "The City That Care Forgot" has somewhat of a derogatory connotation. In

actuality, it refers to the carefree, lackadaisical pace of the city compared to the no-nonsense hurry-up tempo of the northeastern area of the country. The truth of the matter is the fun-loving, working people of the city work very hard and, therefore, utilize the time they have off to the fullest. When they do get to play, they play equally as hard as they work. Chances are, you will not find people anywhere in the country who are more compassionate and caring than the vast majority of the people of the area. The City That Care Forgot just doesn't seem to fit well.

As pointed out, since 1718, New Orleans has had a number of different nicknames to describe it. The one word you will never see used when referring to New Orleans is the word "dull".

JUSTIFIABLE PRIDE

After studying the history of New Orleans over the past 277 years, it is easy to see why citizens can and do stick their chests out with undeniable pride. The reason is as plain as the nose on one's face. Citizens of the Crescent City have

individually and collectively given much to this country and to the world.

As a starter, America's first art form was born in New Orleans. It is called "jazz". No one person invented the music. It was truly a joint musical venture. Jazz was concocted

by using the tempo of the French quadrille and some parts from the opera. Next, church music was added, plus soul music being sung by field hands. Syncopation was thrown in at intervals, along with the African rhythm of the voodoo. All ingredients were then thoroughly mixed, and voila, the foot-stomping, heart-pounding new music spread like wildfire from New Orleans to all corners of the world.

A little-known fact, even by most locals, reference music is that America's first permanent opera company was also

located in New Orleans. Yes, when it comes to culture, New Orleans had it before Dallas, Houston or Atlanta even had agriculture.

The beautiful smiles worn by people of all ages were made possible by a local dentist named Edmund Kells. He is the man credited with inventing dental X-rays. He not only helped us keep our teeth in good shape, he also kept us safe. Other inventions of his were fire extinguishers and elevator brakes, to name just a few of his numerous contributions to mankind.

Another New Orleanian, Etienne de Bore, made life a little sweeter for all of us. He was the first man to success-fully granulate sugar commercially. Could it be New Orleans is the place where the term "How sweet it is!" originated? Millions of housewives around the world love a group of New Orleans chemists without even knowing them. In the 1940's, their ingenious minds invented "perma press". Oops, there goes the old hand iron.

Because of necessity, New Orleans, being geographi-cally located below sea level, its citizens, as a means of self-preservation, built North America's first levees. The U.S. Army Corps of Engineers, after the disastrous 1927 floods, was given the job of building and maintaining levees the en-tire length of the Mississippi River. That is, with the excep-tion of New Orleans. Locals did such a bang-up job building and maintaining its levees, they continued to maintain them up until the late 1950's. New Orleans has the reputation of never having suffered a levee break, nor were they topped, once the crucial height was reached. Another great contribu-tor credited for keeping our city dry was Albert Baldwin Wood. In the late 1800's, he designed, built and installed the largest drainage pumps in the world. No one will deny that he knew what he was doing. The proof of the pudding is in the eating. The pumps are still operating efficiently, keeping the City of New Orleans dry after 100 plus years. Ironically, even though New Orleans has 87 miles of canals that are visible and 85 miles of underground canals, some wide enough for four automobiles to drive through side by side, ironically Venice, Italy, is still called by many around the world the "City of Canals". Venice is given that title even though she has only a paltry 28 miles of canals, and that includes their Grand Canal.

Yes, the Crescent City can boast of having had America's first movie theater, pharmacy, department store, home delivery, electric street car, female editor of a major newspaper, and nationally and internationally renowned female columnist. New Orleans also has the first statue in America dedicated to a female, plus the first female military statue, Molly Marine.

In the area of compassion, I doubt if any other city in North America can come close. The Crescent City is the only city in America with a radio station totally dedicated to the blind and print handicapped. WRBH is on the air 24 hours a day, 365 days a year. The city's Lighthouse for the Blind produces a large percentage of the braille books manufactured in the United States. Through the years, of all major cities that have had bone marrow drives, no  city ever tested over 450 in one day until last year, when New Orleans had close to 900 caring and compassionate people taking the bone marrow test. The above accomplishments are only the tip of the iceberg when talking about the accomplishments and compassion of the people of this great city. As the old adage goes, "It is better to give than receive." Through the years, New Orleanians have gladly and graciously done their part in giving of their time, talents, as well as their financial aid, whenever needed.

YOU ARE GOING TO MOVE WHAT?!

It has been said, and proven time and again, that what one man can dream of, another man, given the necessary funds, can make that dream become a reality. Such is the case in this moving story (please forgive the pun).

In 1935, officials of Louisiana State University Medical Center in New Orleans were having a problem locating a site for a proposed new 17-story dental building. The only available

location for the building was occupied by a $350,000 five-story reinforced-concrete building weighing approximately 10 million pounds. At first, it was thought the 57-foot wide, 105-foot long and 77-foot high (not counting the first floor) brick-covered building would have to be demolished. Since the building was in good condition and facilities it afforded were sorely needed at Charity Hospital, it was decided to move it to a new location 162 feet from where it stood.

Mr. C. Glen Cappel, Vice-President of W. Horace Williams Company, Incorporated, of New Orleans was assigned the project. Test boring at the site showed a satisfactory stratum that was comparatively uniform and could be reached with 45-foot piles. To be extra safe, 15% more piles were driven along the runway and building location. It was felt that the additional 15% would take care of quick loading of

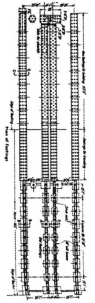

the site. Next on the agenda a cradle was designed, built and installed. As this was being done, 600 six-inch spools turned out of seven-inch steel shafting were being prepared. When completed, each spool weighed 100 pounds. During moving, 342 spools were under the structure at all times. The mode of power for moving the building was supplied by a 10 foot x 12 foot steam engine working through one set of eight-sheave blocks and one set of emergency four-sheave blocks. Six thousand feet of cable were expected to pass over the pulleys 25 times before the building was in its new location.

The day for the big move had finally come on June 4, 1935. In the crowd were city and state officials, including Governor Huey P. Long. He was as proud as a peacock as he strolled around the area greeting everyone. Also in attendance were LSU officials and Leon C. Weiss. Weiss was head of the firm of Weiss, Dreyfous and Seiferth, a New Orleans architectural firm. This was such an important project, it was personally supervised by Mr. Weiss. To his great delight, Roy Cappel, son of C. Glen Cappel, the man who planned and designed the project, was given the dubious distinction of standing on the cradle that held the ten-million-pound load and giving the countdown to start the building on its journey. As soon as young Roy gave the signal, a preliminary pull was initiated with considerable difficulty. All in the audience held their breath. To get the structure in motion, a 615,000-ton (1,230,000,000 pound) pull was needed. As the building slowly moved to its new site, to the cheers of those in attendance, a transit that was set up on a parallel line and sights on cross arms gave continuous readings and levels at both ends of the buildings at the same time. The total elapsed time of moving the massive structure was one hour and 58 minutes. The actual traveling time was 20 minutes, since it was necessary to stop for readjustment of spools and pull cables.

Progress of the building was carefully noted and checked. As the front end of the building went onto the new runway structure, it went down 1/8 of an inch. When the entire building was on the new foundation, the rear of the building went down a corresponding 1/8 of an inch, and the building was then level, in which condition it moved to its final resting place. After the building was free of the run beams and steel supporting structure in the old basement, this steel supporting structure rose 1/4 of an inch.

During the first 24 hours after the building was moved it settled 1/4 of an inch. The next 48 hours showed another 1/4 of an inch settlement. Ten days after the moving, the building apparently came to rest at 3/4 of an inch below its original level. No cracks were visible in any of the plaster or brickwork of the building.

After the building arrived at its final location, the columns were grouted down to the new foundation, all rollers were encased in heavy grease, and then the cradle beams were grouted in leaving the rollers in place, as it was probable that the building would have to be moved again when additional ground was acquired to accommodate the new structures planned for the Charity Hospital.

The engineering marvel was given nation-wide attention by an article written by C. Glen Cappel. In the article, it was pointed out that the move was classified highly successful. Inspection of the building in its new location revealed it was within 1/32 of an inch of its calculated position. The cost to move the structure was only $75,000, a saving of $275,000 to the taxpayers.

As anticipated, the building was once more moved, not to another site, but to its original location. The building was later torn down to make way for the present-day Charity Hospital of Louisiana.

LONGUE VUE
CITY'S LARGEST RESIDENTIAL PROPERTY

The Crescent City has now, and always has had the reputation of having homes built on lots that are so small neighbors can open their windows and shake hands by leaning out of their windows.

Longue Vue is an exception to that rule. In fact, it is the largest piece of residential property in the city. It is located at #7 Bamboo Road on the Jefferson-Orleans line close to Metairie Road.

It is a classical city estate that was the property of the late philanthropist, Edgar Brown Stern, a successful New Orleans cotton broker, and his wife Edith, daughter of Julius Rosenwald, the Sears magnate who was CEO and principal owner with 25% of the company's stock.

The name Longue Vue is derived from the name of a quaint inn on the Hudson River where Mr. Stern's proposal of marriage was made and accepted. During his incredibly active career, Mr. Stern's business interests, including cotton brokerage, were banking, oil, publishing, real estate, as well as being owner and operator of Louisiana's first TV franchise, WDSU TV, and also WDSU Radio.

Following their marriage in 1921, the young couple purchased a piece of land adjacent to the New Orleans Country Club. A large, comfortable, colonial-style house was built on

a lot measuring 250 by 500 feet. Additional land was purchased, eventually totaling eight acres. Having a keen interest in horticulture, Mrs. Stern engaged the nationally renowned landscape architect, Ellen Biddle Shipman, to design and lay out gardens on the entire property. Before this was done, numerous trips to Europe to study the most beautiful and better-known gardens were made. When the plans were approved and the gardens completed, Mrs. Stern was almost completely satisfied. There was one small burr under his saddle of satisfaction. The newly created gardens left the house behind. By that, we mean the gardens lay mostly to the south of the house. There were very few views of the garden when one was in the house. With necessary financing available, the dilemma was easily corrected. The decision was made to move the house and custom design and build another that would offer a view of the fabulous garden, no matter which of the 45 rooms (includes baths, and closets) one was in.

The original home was ingeniously moved by mules with the aid of winches and cypress logs. The house today is located on the corner lot of Metairie Road and Garden Lane.

To be guaranteed that their dream house would take full advantage of the gardens by bringing the outdoors indoors, and at the same time be architecturally acceptable, the eminent architect, William Platt, was contacted. After discussing the project, Mr. Platt enthusiastically accepted the challenge. He spent the next four years devoting the bulk of his energies completing the contract. The Sterns particularly admired Louisiana Greek revival architecture. They took William and his brother Geoffrey, who was also to work on the unique project, to visit various parts of Louisiana to see the architectural styles they most admired. The final design included a combination of the following structures. The eastern elevation is based on Shadows-on-the-Teche in New Iberia. The south and west elevations are similar to Le Charpentier-Beauregard House in the French Quarter.

Longue Vue was one of the last great houses to be custom built in America. To be sure that every detail was guar-

 anteed perfection, the mill work was made to specifications in New York and shipped to New Orleans. Window sashes were made of mahogany. Sections of the painted mill work are birch and mahogany. Doors in the formal rooms are of Honduran mahogany. Floors of brick set in the popular Louisiana herringbone pattern were installed, along with wooden floors that included Brazilian rosewood veneer-planking, pine, and quartered oak strips.

Plaster details such as cornices, moulding and ceiling centerpieces were all produced by Angelo Angelose in New York.

Every small detail, no matter how minute, was painstakingly studied before artisans finally did the work. Even though the house was air-conditioned from its inception, it was felt fresh air while dining was more enjoyable. To be sure the gardens, as well as fresh air, could be made a part of the dining experience, the center panes were made to lower into the basement. Screens could then be raised in their place, allowing fresh air to enter the room.

Other niceties of the house included a room just for wrapping packages and gifts. Another was allocated to making floral arrangements. So that the arranger could see what the creation looked like from all angles while working, mirrors were strategically placed.

True, the house is unique and possibly unequaled anywhere in the city; yet the highlight of Longue Vue is the massive grounds and meticulously planned and groomed gardens. To provide a cooling effect in the gardens, 23 beautiful and diversified fountains can be found sprinkling throughout the

grounds. They are as different as the perennial flowers that grace the gardens at different times of the year. To achieve perfection, eight full-time gardeners work year round keeping the grounds groomed. The chief gardener lives on the premises.

During their lives, Mr. and Mrs. Stern gave of their talents, leadership and finances for the good of the city. For their efforts, each received the coveted Times-Picayune Loving Cup, the only husband and wife to ever do so. The cups are prominently displayed in the drawing room at Longue

Vue.

It was not surprising that one of Mrs. Stern's final philanthropic gestures was the creation of a non-profit foundation to maintain her home and beautiful gardens. Until this day, it is by far the largest and possibly most unique residential property in the entire city.

HOW DRY I AM
OR
ALLIGATORS UP TO THE ARMPITS

Dry, New Orleans is not. You can wet your whistle with liquid libation any time of the day on any day of the year, at any one of the many drinking establishments sprinkled generously throughout the city.

Dry, New Orleans is not, with almost 60 inches of annual rainfall.

Dry, New Orleans is not, with more than one half of the 365 square miles of the city covered by swamps, marshes, prairies, bayous, rivers and canals, both man-made for drainage and those created by God. New Orleans East alone has 182 square miles covered by water in one way or another.

Because of these conditions, the city is credited, good or bad depending on how you look at it, with having more alligators living within the city limits than any other major city in the country, or the world, for

that matter.

Prior to the founding of New Orleans, the Indians called the area "Chinchuba", meaning alligator. In 1726, Jean Pierre La Sassus completed the earliest known painting of New Orleans. Prominently shown in the drawing (looking at New Orleans from the Westbank) is a man shoving a pole down the mouth of a huge alligator. On June 18, 1852, when the city got around to designing an official seal, you guessed it, an alligator was prominently displayed. In fact, it was the largest single image on the seal.

GUESTIMATE NUMBER OF ALLIGATORS IN CITY LIMITS

New Orleans East alone, as mentioned, has 182 square miles of canals or marshes, etc. When alligators were on the endangered species, it was estimated there were five pairs per square mile. This would make the population in New Orleans East alone 1,820. With each alligator laying 35-75 eggs, the average being 55 eggs per year, and losing 50% of the crop, they would still produce 25,000 alligators in just one year. The endangered species, without anyone other than man recognized as a predator, it is easy to understand that within a relatively short period of time, unless they are thinned out, we would literally be up to our armpits in these nasty critters.

EIGHTEEN
WHITE ALLIGATORS

Not only were the 18 white alligators found in a nest by three Louisiana Cajun fishermen on Louisiana Land & Ex-

ploration property near Houma, Louisiana, in August of 1987 the first such find anywhere in the world, they were also the only ones ever found. All 18 are male. This is not uncommon, since the sex of baby alligators is determined by the water temperature of the nest.

They are not merely an oddity, but an extraordinary oddity, for they are white, but not albinos. Albinos are white with pinkish eyes. These alligators, would you believe, have blue eyes. This makes them leucism, which is even more rare than albinos.

Having been found on LL&E property, they became the property of LL&E. Soon after being found, four were graciously donated to the Audubon Zoo. The remainder are being raised by LL&E on an alligator farm. Today, the farm-raised white alligators average eight feet long and 250 pounds each. They grow much, much faster than those kept in the zoo, which average 5 feet long and 50-60 pounds each.

Their uniqueness has made these critters famous world wide. They have appeared on virtually every major TV network in the U.S., as well as overseas. At times, a few of these truly unique creatures are loaned out to other zoos around the world. Wherever they go, they attract people like bees are attracted to honey.

Watch out Frank Sinatra; when people make reference to "Old Blue Eyes" today, they could be speaking not of the human crooner, but of the thousands of young and old who croon when they see these beautiful white alligators with blue eyes.

PICTURES DON'T LIE
IT WAS BIG

In 1982, photographer Charles W. Frank, Butch Jeanfreau and Joe Billiot were in a small boat in the Honey Island Swamp. Joe Billiot latched onto an enormous alligator. It dragged the boat and passengers around and around like a toy for what seemed like an eternity before Charles Frank shot it in the head. When winched into the boat, it measured 13 feet, 6 inches in length, with a girth of 8 feet, 6 inches. It

was 1-1/2 feet longer than the boat. Even though there wasn't a scale to weigh the critter, chances are it weighed more than the boat and passengers combined. It was one of the largest alligators ever taken in Louisiana.

IN ITS DAY COTTON WAS KING

If you were asked to choose one commodity or product that elevated New Orleans to the top of the economic ladder in the 19th century, it would be, without a close rival, cotton. True, it was known to have been planted in Louisiana as early as 1718, the same year New Orleans was founded. But, like every other port in the United States, and the rest of the world for that matter, it was not a profitable commodity until the end of the 18th century when Eli Whitney invented the cotton gin. When it finally took off, it surged like a rocket headed to the moon. By 1809, cotton was being grown in greater and greater quantities to supply the world's demand. With this new demand, New Orleans became the world's leading cotton exporting port. Because of cotton, New Orleans gained the distinction of being one of the three great cotton contract markets in the world.

The first recorded shipment of cotton from the North American continent (Charlotte, North Carolina) to the world's market (London, England) took place in 1784 and consisted of only six bags. In a short time, production increased to seven million bales a year. Cotton became the number one export product from North America and quickly exceeded all other exported items in dollar value.

This all came about because of two great inventions. One was the cotton gin by Eli Whitney, allowing, for the first time, the economic processing of cotton after it was picked. The other invention was the steamboat, invented by Robert Fulton, that made possible fast and economical transportation of the new commodity that was white in color, but, some historians say, equal to gold in value.

By the 1930s, Louisiana, along with Mississippi, was producing 500,000 bales annually. New Orleans had, by that time, a half-dozen steam-operated cotton presses that compressed the cotton into bales so that they would take up less space in shipping, thereby reducing the overhead and increasing the gross profit.

The largest cotton press in New Orleans in 1830 was the New Orleans Cotton Press. It was two blocks in length with a capacity of 150,000 bales annually. In addition to the cotton presses, there was a storage facility for 25,000 bales.

Because of the vast quantity of cotton that came through New Orleans, by the middle 1800s, the Port of New Orleans had the reputation of being the most-efficiently operated port to be found anywhere. The following is a good example. The J. M. White Steamboat arrived in the Port of New Orleans a little after 6:00 a.m. with 6,000 bales of cotton and 4,000 sacks of cotton seeds. By 11:45 a.m., the ship was completely unloaded and by 5:00 p.m., was reloaded and ready to sail with a return cargo.

Cotton brought untold wealth to the South, especially Louisiana. Three consecutive successful crops could and did make millionaires. Before the Civil War, Louisiana had more millionaires than all the other states combined.

The dark clouds of the Civil War put a damper on the

cotton trade like all other trade. After the war ended, the cotton trade started up again and gradually regained its rightful place in world trade.

In 1871, the New Orleans Cotton Exchange was founded by 18 cotton merchants to facilitate and regulate trading. Cotton was king and now had its own trading room that became outgrown in just ten years. On May 12, 1883, with an active membership of over 600 members, a new $400,000.00 Cotton Exchange Building, complete with elevators, was dedicated. The New Orleans guide book stated, "The new Cotton Exchange Building is considered by many the handsomest and most graceful building in the city. The exchange room is situated on the ground floor and extends from Carondelet Street to Variety Alley, a distance of 100 feet in length and a width of 50 feet. There is perhaps no room on this side of the Atlantic on the embellishment of which so much time and pains have been expended." (This was followed by one-and-a-half pages of description of art works, sculptured frescoes and other ornamentations.)

Just as cotton had catapulted the South to the forefront economically before the Civil War, cotton was to be used as the instrument to help pull the South out of the economic slump brought on by the occupation forces after the war.

At a meeting in Birmingham, Alabama, made up of cotton brokers from all over the South, it was decided that a new slogan, "The New South", would be the rallying point. The vehicle used to convey the new slogan was to be a World's Fair celebrating the 100th anniversary of the exporting of cotton to the world's market. At the same meeting, it was decided the best possible location would be the number one cotton port city, New Orleans, Louisiana. The official name for the fair was, "The World's Industrial and Cotton Centennial Exposition". Although the fair itself was not a financial success, the slogan selected, "The New South," was achieved.

With advanced technology and introduction of many, many synthetic products, the one-time gluttonous demand for cotton had passed. But, the glory days when cotton was king will never be forgotten.

A few things that are still part of New Orleans' culture bear mentioning, as they were instituted by men who were cotton brokers in New Orleans.

A group of six young men from Mobile, Alabama, working as cotton brokers in New Orleans, were the leaders of a group of 83 men who organized, in 1857, the Krewe of Comus -- the oldest Mardi Gras marching club in North America.

A group of young men from England, working as cotton brokers in New Orleans, introduced to the city in 1874 a game called tennis. The New Orleans Lawn Tennis Club was dedicated on December 15, 1876, and is the oldest tennis club in North America.

And, of course, Press Street takes its name from all the important cotton presses of long ago.

THE GOOD OLD DAYS!!!

It has been stated, not by a few but by many, that there is no such time as the "good old days". For the vast majority, today, yesterday and possibly last week were and are the good old days.

One typical example is the telephones. In 1896, 20 years after the instrument was invented, only a fraction of 1% of the businesses and residences had the luxury of owning and using telephones. In the 1940's, my family did have the good fortune of having a telephone and the misfortune of being on a five-party line. This was done not because a private line was unavailable but because of financial need to keep the cost down. Besides the inconvenience of slow rotary dialing, we were restricted to using the unit only when one of the other four parties was not on the line. Of course, this inconvenience did provide a little entertainment. You could, and sometimes did, listen in on your party line's conversation. True, in

1940's—Multitudes of telephone subscribers were still using two and four party line service.

those days, you were required to call only six numbers or letters, whereas today, everyone has a seven-digit number. It really doesn't matter today how many numbers you must dial, for most units have last-number redial or predial numbers that require only two numbers to reach your party. Other present conveniences are such things as answering machines, records that tell you the number and name of the party calling before you pick up the phone, call forwarding, call waiting, etc.

For the present generation, an explanation of the term used above of numbers and letters is as follows. Today, we use numbers only. For many years, each area of the city was divided into sections, with each section having an exchange name that was abbreviated by using two letters.

Exchanges used through the years were:

BYwater, TUlane, FIlmore, CHestnut, HUnter, JAckson, RAymond, CAnal, etc.

The newest entry into mass communications for the convenience of its user is the cellular phone. Cellular phones work the same as telephones, with the exception being they are portable and can be used anywhere as long as the instrument is in range of a cell site. The telephone, as we all know, works through wires, whereas cellular is wireless. Cellular can be used anywhere, including in the middle of a swamp, at a remote hunting lodge, in your automobile, golf cart, boat or wherever cell sites offer coverage.

To show the phenomenal growth of this new form of communication, the telephone generated 600,000 users in its first 20 years of existence. Cellular communications began in 1984, and by 1994 close to 20 million units were in use.

From this one piece of information, one could surmise, reference communication, today and tomorrow are the good old days. And guess what? They are going to get even better. The once-thought-of way-out Dick Tracy wrist watch telephone is right around the corner.

PARKS
MASSIVE, HUMONGOUS AND ITSY BITSY, TEENY WEENY

New Orleans is blessed with numerous parks scattered throughout the city. Beautiful City Park is by far the largest in the city, as well as the fifth largest in the United States.

The land the park occupies was once the Allard Plantation. John McDonogh, the famous philanthropist, purchased it at an auction and gave it to the city. In doing so, he thought they would subdivide the land and sell it for residential sites. This, he felt, would allow the city to fatten its meager coffers. The city fathers had other ideas.

City Park has hundreds of benches on which people rest in the shade of thousands and thousands of trees. The park is blessed with acres of recreation for the citizens, including horseback riding, scores of softball diamonds, two football stadiums, fishing, boating, picnic areas, and, would you believe, four 18-hole golf courses all within one park. The park is massive enough that a walker would take hours to complete a full lap around its perimeter.

Not far from the humongous City Park is the city's smallest. Because it fronted DeSoto Street, it is officially listed as DeSoto Park. The triangular park is surrounded by Crete Street, DeSoto Street and Esplanade Avenue. A short distance away is North Broad Street. The park measures four feet across at the narrow end, and 146 feet on the wide end. The disecting sides are 425 feet on Esplanade and 448 feet on DeSoto.

This tiny park is just the opposite of City Park in its origin. It was residential land donated to the city for a park by Mr. Louis Jung after he completed construction of his beautiful home in 1896. With ample grounds for his own enjoyment, he graciously made the land occupied by the small park a gift to the city for the enjoyment of his neighbors.

The huge home is of a classic style with Corinthian columns and an uncommon wooden upper gallery with a railing fretted with Oriental designs. Mr. Jung founded the Jung and Sons Coal Company. He had his own coal harbor and a fleet of 70 barges on the Mississippi River. The home built by Mr. Jung has one other unique feature for a city built below sea level. It has a cellar that houses the boiler which provided steam heat.

DeSoto Park, with no benches and only one tall palm tree, is small enough that a walker could circle its perimeter in less than a minute. No doubt, the city fathers felt the person would not be tired enough to require a bench to rest.

City Park and DeSoto Park are both functional in their own rights. It is ironic that City Park's property was purchased by John McDonogh with the understanding that it would be used for residential purposes. On the other hand, Louis Jung purchased the land to build a residence. He had sufficient grounds for his own use and donated a little piece of land that is now DeSoto Park.

ICEBERGS FLOAT PAST NEW ORLEANS

For an event to outdraw a Mardi Gras parade in New Orleans, it has to be something extra spectacular.

Such an event began on Friday, February 17, 1899, and ended four days later. For the first time in recorded history, large ice formations were seen floating past Canal Street. These were not small chunks of ice but pieces estimated anywhere from 12 to 24 inches thick and 20 to 100 feet in diameter, with some even larger. The packed ice, with water sprayed from the winds, piled one layer atop another which

formed weird and wonderful shapes that had 9/10 of the near 300,000 population lining the levee on both sides of the river, saying with excitement in their voices, "Look at that one, no look at that one, wow! Would you look at that one?" A description given by one of the spectators viewing the phenomenon was that it looked like a big field of dirty cotton.

Most steamboat captains feared the consequences of running paddlewheel craft through ice and tied up their boats until the phenomenon passed. Two excursion boats, the Sunrise and America, with a combined 300 passengers who came to New Orleans for Mardi Gras, delayed their departure until it was safe.

The skipper of the Canal St. ferry, on the other hand, did not discontinue river crossings. On Sunday, February 19, 1899, 8,000 brave Orleanians threw caution to the winds and took what they knew would be a ride of a lifetime. The ferry captain masterfully maneuvered his small craft cautiously through occasional breaks in the ice. When the boat collided with chunks of ice, the noisy crowd would become as quiet as a church mouse, and, once the ice went by, the noise level went back to a feverish pitch.

Yes, it was a day to remember, one that was truly chilling, especially for people who live in a semi-tropical climate.

GENERAL LAFAYETTE
AMERICAN FREEDOM FIGHTER

New Orleans has always had a flair for welcoming special guests to the city, and the reception of Marie Joseph Paul Yves Roch Gilbert du Montier, Marquis de Lafayette, was no exception. Although he had declined the invitation to be the state's first governor when the United States purchased Louisiana, his popularity had not diminished.

In preparation for his visit, the city government decided to go to extremes befitting a Frenchman of such rank. The famous and much-used city

hall, the Cabildo, was emptied completely of its contents and redecorated as Lafayette's residence for his six-day visit. From this vantage point, he would be able to view and appreciate the surprise planned for Place d'Armes (later Jackson Square) in his honor.

A noted military leader who had so greatly aided the Americans in their fight for freedom, Lafayette was greeted at the site of the Battle of New Orleans in Chalmette by Louisiana Governor Henry S. Johnson and other leading citizens of the state. From there, a large parade made its way into the city, where an anxious, enormous crowd was waiting patiently with New Orleans Mayor Louis Philippe de Roffignac, who was to officially welcome the Marquis de Lafayette to the city.

When the parade headed by the Marquis came into view, church bells began pealing as the horde waved handkerchiefs and chanted, "Vive Lafayette, vive Lafayette". The closer he came the louder they cheered, and the more enthusiastically they waved their handkerchiefs. When the Marquis reached Place d'Armes, a salute was fired, which sounded like a battalion of cannons. Here on foreign soil he was being treated like a demigod.

In tribute, City Engineer J. Pilie had been instructed by city fathers to design a replica of the Arc de Triomphe. The 68-foot high, 58-foot wide, 25-foot deep replica, painted to look like green marble, was constructed by J. B. Fogliardi. On the base were painted figures representing justice and liberty. Adorning the arch were two allegorical forms with trumpets and ribands depicting fame and bearing the names of Washington and Lafayette. At the very top, was a statue representing wisdom above a bust of Benjamin Franklin.

Mayor Roffignac was standing under the arch ready to welcome Lafayette to the city, but the clapping and shouting was deafening. So, he simply pointed to an inscription which read in both French and English, "A grateful republic consecrates this monument to Lafayette."

The 68-year-old Marquis de Lafayette, immortal French patriot and hero of three revolutions, was treated in the manner New Orleans felt he deserved.

Out of sight, out of mind did not hold true in his case; he was not forgotten after his visit in 1825. Three Faubourgs (subdivisions) - Annunciation, Livaudais and Lafayette - were incorporated in 1833 by a Legislative Act as the City of Lafayette. Lafayette consisted of 14,000 people, a cemetery, railway, newspaper, fire department and its own still-existing Lafayette Square, located directly across from the old City Hall (now called Gallier Hall).

The City of Lafayette was finally absorbed into the City of New Orleans in 1852, but, as if in recompense, the name of Vermilion City in Southwest Louisiana was changed to the City of Lafayette, which is now the oil capital of Louisiana.

THE NEW ORLEANS PELICANS

In 1870, the Cincinnati Redlegs, the nation's first professional baseball club, went on a cross-country tour of the United States. New Orleans was one of the many stops along the way. The first of the five games scheduled in New Orleans was played on April 25th and was against the New Orleans Pelicans. This was the first team to bear the Pelican label in the print media. The game wasn't even close. The New Orleans Pelicans lost 51-1. The team had nothing to be ashamed of though, for over a two-year period, the Redlegs won 126 games and lost only six (.955 avg.). The Redlegs scored over 100 runs five times during this period. You can easily say the Redlegs were virtually a scoring machine. Of the five New Orleans games (Cincinnati won all five), they scored a whopping 219 runs, the opponents a measly 24.

100th ANNIVERSARY

On April 17, 1887, the New Orleans Pelicans professional team made its debut. As a member of the Southern League, they defeated Mobile, Alabama, 5-2. With 75 wins and only 40 losses (.652 avg.), they went on to win the pennant in their first year in the league.

From the opening game in 1887 to the final game in 1977, the New Orleans Pelicans brought many hours of enjoyment to thousands of metropolitan New Orleans baseball fans. 1987 marked the 100th anniversary of the first New Orleans Pelicans professional baseball team.

ROUGH START

In 1888, the Pelicans played in both the Southern League and the Texas League; both folded before the season ended.

GOLDEN ERA

From 1901 through 1938, the Pelicans finished in the first division all but five times. During that golden period, ten pennants proudly flew atop the stadium.

INNOVATIVE

The father of Louisiana baseball, Abner Powell, gave to the game not only ladies day, the rain check and the infield cover (he got the idea from watching stevedores cover cotton bales on the waterfront with tarpaulins); he was also the first man in baseball history to steal home on the pitcher's wind-up.

IRON MAN MOXIE

Perhaps the most phenomenal "Iron-Man" stunt ever pulled by a pitcher who wore the flannels of the New Orleans Pelicans happened in New Orleans on June 15, 1907. "Moxie"

Manuel pitched and won a double-header against Birmingham. Both were nine-inning games that he won by identical 1-0 scores. In both games he gave up a total of only eight hits, two in the first game and six in the second.

"Iron-Man Moxie" was really in the groove that day. He did not allow a single base on balls in either game, plus he struck out a total of 11 men in the two games. To top off the phenomenal evening, the first game was played in 1-1/2 hours, and the second was completed in one hour and 32 minutes.

EDDIE ROSE

At the plate, he fouled the ball like a man with uncontrollable hiccups.

An unusual record in the Pelicans record book is held by outfielder Eddie Rose. On July 9, 1934, playing against Knoxville in Knoxville, he stepped up to the plate, and with a count of 2-2, proceeded to foul off three straight pitches. Hulvey, the Knoxville pitcher, directed a few unkind remarks towards home plate about lazy batters. Eddie took the snide remarks as a personal insult, and, for the next 16 pitches, he swung and fouled each. It wasn't until the 17th toss that he grounded out to the infield.

Although Eddie Rose was out on this play, he was in the record books. Nineteen consecutive fouls by Eddie Rose stands till this day in the New Orleans Pelicans record book.

On August 12th, 1935, Eddie Rose gained national acclaim by killing a pigeon with a pop fly.

DID YOU KNOW?

An early rule in baseball stated the following: To determine who would be at bat first, a coin would be tossed with the winner being able to select coming to bat first. This of course was a definite advantage, for only one ball was used for the entire game. As the game went on, the ball got softer, and softer, and softer.

LAST BASEBALL GAME
PELICAN STADIUM

The last baseball game to be played at the old New Orleans Pelican Stadium occurred on Sunday, September 1, 1957. The Pelicans had furnished fond memories at this lo-

cation dating back to April 13, 1915, when the site was officially opened after having been moved piecemeal from Banks
and Carrollton by mules and then reconstructed at the Tulane
and Carrollton location as Heinemann Park.

The date September 1, 1957, was one literally filled with
crocodile tears. Not only did the New Orleans Pelicans lose
to Memphis in this season finale, by a score of 7 to 3, to make
matters worse, only 941 fans, who appeared to be in shock,
were in attendance to bid a fond farewell to the players and
the ballpark. The final batter in the historic game was Dick
Klinesmith. Just as the rest of the day went, he grounded out
in the role of a pinch hitter, as Bill Darden, a Memphis right
hander, threw the last pitch in the old park.

Robert Jarvis, Pelican left fielder of the day, etched his
name in the baseball history book of Pelican Stadium by hitting a solo homer in the ninth inning, last home run ever to be
hit in the stadium. It came off southpaw Bill Hendry, who
was the last pitcher to win a ballgame there.

Harry "Peanuts" Lowrey was the last manager at the old
site. As manager, he could do what he felt best for the team.

So, he inserted himself into the lineup that Sunday afternoon as a pinch hitter. He batted for pitcher Walt Kellner in the eighth. You guessed it...he struck out.

Not only was the last game played at Pelican Stadium a losing one, the entire season was disastrous. The 1957 Pelicans finished last, five games behind the seventh-place Little Rock Travelers. Besides losing the game and finishing last in the league, the final nail in the coffin was in the form of only 66,151 fans making it to the Pelican games for the entire season.

As you study the box scores for the final game at Pelican Stadium, you learn that in spite of their record, there were some outstanding ball players on the team. Russell Snider, the Pel lead-off man, went on to the majors and played twelve seasons of big league ball, including three games in the 1966 World Series. Although Harry "Peanuts" Lowrey, the manager of the Pelicans in that last game, struck out, he did have an excellent major league career that spanned from 1942 to 1955, appearing as an outfielder for the Chicago Cubs who played in the World Series in 1945. Wayne Belardi, first baseman for the Pelicans, played six years of major league ball, spanning from 1950 through 1956. Morris Thacker, a pinch hitter in that last game, went on to the majors, playing five years in the National League. Pitcher Steve Kraly, who played in the final game, also played in the majors.

BASEBALL PARKS IN NEW ORLEANS
WHERE PROFESSIONAL GAMES WERE PLAYED

SPORTSMAN PARK - 1887
City Park Avenue & present-day Pontchartrain Expressway

ATHLETIC PARK - 1901
Tulane Avenue between S. Carrollton and S. Pierce
PELICAN PARK - 1908
S. Carrollton between Banks and Palmyra
HEINEMANN PARK - 1915
Tulane & S. Carrollton Avenues
CITY PARK STADIUM - 1958, 1959 - City Park
LOUISIANA SUPERDOME - 1977

UNIVERSITY OF NEW ORLEANS - 1994

CONTROVERSIAL MONUMENT

New Orleans' beloved Canal Street, ever since its birth in 1807, has been the location of multitudes of joyous occasions.

At the other end of the spectrum, on September 14, 1874, Canal Street was the location for one of the saddest events in the city's history. The circumstances leading up to that fatal day were as follows.

Although New Orleans was the largest city in the Confederate States of America without fortifications, sufficient troops and arms to defend itself, it was the first major city in the Civil War to fall into Federal hands (April 1862). General Butler, known as "Spoons Butler" because of the silverware he confiscated, upon occupying New Orleans quickly became an unpopular man. His popularity continued to diminish, especially after he issued controversial General Order Number 28 which directed his soldiers to treat any female, who by word or gesture insulted federal soldiers, as "women of the town".

After the war ended, carpetbag rule (or misrule, as most Louisianians claimed) was the beginning of the darkest days in Louisiana's political history. During these turbulent times, taxes increased 500%, and services were nil. Prewar legislative sessions cost less than $100,000.00; carpetbag legislative sessions exceeded one million dollars. The state debt prior to the war was six million. In short order, the state debt rose to 50 million dollars. Because of the blatant misuse of state funds, Louisiana was bankrupt and could not even pay the interest on its debt. Governor Henry Clay Warmoth, a carpetbagger from Illinois, with a salary of only $8,000 a year, amassed a fortune at a phenomenal rate. His indiscretions were so blatant, he was impeached. President Ulysses S. Grant replaced him with a temporary governor named P. B. S. Pinchback. Pinchback became the first black man in the history of the United States to serve as governor of any state.

In the next gubernatorial election, John McEnery, a liberal Louisiana Democrat, ran against a Vermont carpetbagger named William Pitt Kellogg. Even though McEnery received seven thousand more votes than Kellogg, Kellogg was declared "Elected" by the radical returning board. Although Louisiana citizens thought things had gotten as bad as they could, they were in for the shock of their lives as conditions deteriorated even further. As the New York Tribune printed a few years later, Louisiana's legislature was filled with thieves, adventurers, barbers, bootblacks, bartenders and confidence men. Offices were sold to the highest bidders. Business was brought to the point that nothing could be bought or sold, except votes.

In north Louisiana in the small town of Coushatta, the people rioted en masse in 1874 when they learned arms of all private citizens in Louisiana were to be confiscated. Under this order, Louisiana would be the only state where a man could not walk the streets carrying a gun. Next, Governor

Kellogg issued an order to intercept and seize the Steamboat Mississippi as she headed to New Orleans carrying guns and ammunition. This action precipitated the gathering on September 14, 1874, of the members of the White League of Louisiana. They met on the neutral ground on Canal and St. Charles Streets by the statue of Henry Clay. Kellogg's abdication was asked for and unanswered, leading to the crowd's determination to drive out the usurper. At approximately 2:30

p.m., the White League and Kellogg's metropolitan police began what was labeled in the newspaper, "The Battle of Liberty Place". The battle involved thousands of men on each side. Each side had rifles, machine guns and cannons. When Kellogg's metropolitan police were finally driven out, losses to the White League were 16 killed, 45 wounded. The casualties of the metropolitan police were 11 killed, 60 wounded. Although the White League won the battle, President Ulysses S. Grant restored order and returned the government to Kellogg after sending 5,000 federal troops to Louisiana.

On November 15, 1882, an ordinance was passed by the City Council dedicating the neutral ground on Canal Street between Wells and Delta Streets (location where fighting was the heaviest) for the erection of a monument. The area would be known as Liberty Place.

The cornerstone for the monument was laid on September 14, 1899. Chiseled into the monument are the names of the 16 men from Louisiana who were killed in the battle. The monument has the following inscription: "In honor of those who fell in defense of civil liberty and home rule in that heroic and successful struggle of the 14th of September, 1874".

CAUSE OF CONTROVERSY

For years, the monument served its original purpose. The ruckus only began when an unauthorized inscription was added while it was in storage during renovations being made to the neutral ground where it stood. The new inscription made reference to white supremacy. In spite of the monument's original purpose, having absolutely nothing to do with race supremacy, when the volatile inscription was added both the KKK and the NAACP rallied around the statue on behalf of their individual causes.

A comparison of how meaningless the controversy over the monument is, compare it theoretically to an unauthorized inscription reference black supremacy being placed on the Martin Luther King monument. Even though everyone knows Martin Luther King sought equality, not black supremacy, chances are if an unauthorized black supremacy inscription were added, it, too, could possibly lead to controversy.

LITTLE KNOWN FACTS

More Americans were killed at the infamous Battle of Liberty Place than at the famous Battle of New Orleans.

THIS COULD NOT HAPPEN TODAY

A virtually unknown young army private named Edward Douglas White, as a member of the White League, took part in the battle. In later years, he became Chief Justice of The United States Supreme Court.

DAUGHTERS OF CHARITY

In 1581, in the small town of Pouy in the south of France, a son was born into the de Paul family. Vincent, as he was named, had more than ordinary intelligence, wit, sense of discipline and charm of personality. Early in life, he chose the priesthood for his vocation. After ordination, he spent four years at the university to earn his degree in theology. In his early years in the priesthood, Vincent became obsessed with worldly comforts and possessions. But this was to change and change drastically. On a voyage to Toulouse, his ship was captured by pirates, and all of those captured were sold into slavery. After some years, he did manage to escape. With his new freedom, he once again became obsessed, this time with helping those in need. There were many, for he lived during the French Civil War and the Thirty Years' War.

Vincent was bright enough to realize that he could not accomplish all that needed to be done by himself. He convinced the ladies of Europe, mostly women with families, that they should go to the streets, hospitals, jails, and wherever there was a need to help those less fortunate than themselves. He proved to be a fantastic and tireless motivator. As he organized a group and they became efficient, he moved into the next city. He organized what he called "The Ladies of Charity" throughout Europe. In a sense, you could say that Vincent is credited with being the first to franchise works of charity (as hamburgers, fried chicken, and pizza pies are today). One day, he realized just how much more could be accomplished if he could organize young women to dedicate their entire lives to work for charity. In 1633, Vincent met Louise de Marillac, and together they formed the first female religious order of its kind in the world, calling them "The Daughters of Charity". What made them different from all other female religious orders was that The Daughters of Charity would not be cloistered (confined behind walls); rather, they would, like The Ladies of Charity, go into the streets, especially the slum areas. They could also be found in the battlefields, in the prisons, as well as in hospitals and schools. They soon became a symbol of mercy, recognized by men and women of every religious denomination. With this new approach to helping the less fortunate, the Daughters soon became the stuff of which legends are made. The works of The Daughters of Charity spread like a plague throughout Europe.

DAUGHTERS OF CHARITY IN NORTH AMERICA

At the time of the Louisiana Purchase in 1803, the population of New Orleans was only 8,052. By 1830, the population had reached 49,826. Many of the new arrivals lived in what was called the American sector. The great majority were in dire need of assistance of every conceivable kind. Bishop Rosati (third Bishop of New Orleans) remembered the fantastic work of The Daughters of Charity both in Europe and the U.S. (Mother Seton was the founder of The Daughters of Charity in the United States in 1813). He requested, on April 19, 1829, that they send sisters to help with the tremendous needs of the community. They responded by sending Sisters Regina and Magdalen from their mother house in St. Louis. The good sisters were accompanied by their superior as far as Baltimore, and the rest of the slow voyage was made on their own. The good sisters left Baltimore on December 29,

SISTER REGINA & SISTER MAGDALEN
ARRIVE NEW ORLEANS JAN. 6, 1830

1829, and arrived in New Orleans on January 30, 1830. Bishop Rosati assigned them to start a school for colored girls and to adminster the female orphan asylum. In addition to the assignments issued by Bishop Rosati, the sisters also administered to the poor and the sick. In 1831, five more Daughters of Charity joined the original two. Their reputation of deep compassion, hard work and exceptional administrative abilities soon spread throughout the city. They were tireless in their work, beginning at 4:30 a.m., and ending with night prayers at 8:30 p.m. Since all work and no play makes for a dull bunny, the sisters had one half hour of recreation each night before prayers. Because of the reputation they had built in a very short time that they were in New Orleans, they were asked to immediately take over managment of the internal economy of Charity Hospital. On January 16, 1834, eight months after the request, Sister Regina and nine other sisters entered the hospital. After 161 years, their successors are still tireless workers in the institution.

Over the years, The Daughters of Charity have labored in numerous orphan asylums, schools and hospitals, including the Leper Hospital at Carville. Their most recent project is at Ozanam Inn, where they daily assist feeding and housing the homeless.

The Daughters of Charity have worked tirelessly for 356 years in Europe and over 180 years in New Orleans. The reason for their longevity is that they have been able to change with the times. Just as the dress of the members has changed over the years, so, too, The Daughters of Charity have been able to change with the times. It is a known fact that today there are not as many members in the order as in past years. Yet, when you combine members of The Daughters of Charity with the laity who work with them, the combined numbers of their accomplishments are greater than ever before.

Just as back in the 1500's when Vincent realized that he couldn't do it on his own and asked others to help, today The Daughters of Charity, with fewer in number, realize that they can not do it all on their own, and are asking for help, and help is coming in bushel baskets.

On his death bed at age 79, Vincent de Paul was visited by Queen Anne, mother of Louis XIV, who had been a friend of Vincent for years. She truly loved him and came to bid him a final goodbye. During their final dialogue, these words were exchanged: "Monsieur Vincent", the Queen began, "you have lived your life well. You have fed the hungry, clothed the naked, healed the sick, visited those in prison, comforted the afflicted. Tell me, is there anything left for you to do?" "Yes, madame", the old man replied. "Tell me what it is," the worried Queen asked. "More." It was with this one word Vincent expressed the perfect epitaph of his life, and the life of every Daughter of Charity in the world.

PULITZER BROTHERS NECK WEAR COMPANY WEMBLEY WEMCO TIE TYCOON OF THE WORLD

On July 1, 1925, brothers Sam and Emanuel Pulitzer, 20 and 22 years, respectively, decided to team up and make their mark in the business world. Their difficult early lives served to temper them for the cruel and sometimes difficult business arena they were ready to enter. With very little formal education, little experience and even less money

($300.00), they formed The Pulitzer Brothers Neckwear Company. The basis of their entering this line of business was that Emanuel had worked in New York and had gained some expertise in the sale of neck ties.

Although their business experience was nil, they both had learned from their parents the importance of hard work tempered with scheduled time for relaxation. Above all, they were taught the importance of dealing fairly with all people at all times.

In 1925, bow ties were the craze. The company purchased them from a manufacturer in New York and the brothers, full of enthusiasm, blanketed every town in south Louisiana. The first month they each earned $60.00. The brothers were on cloud nine. That is, until they learned the meaning of cash flow. Their selling skills outshined their customers' capacity to pay timely. They also learned the harsh reality of borrowing money. Through dedication and persistence, they overcame these two giant obstacles. In 1928, the next step in the growth plan took shape in the opening of their own manufacturing facility. The plant slowly grew to a staff of thirty. Once again, cash flow's ugly head raised itself. Because of fair dealings with their employees and the unbelievable loyalty of their customers and suppliers, once again they were able to prevail. By 1929, the company outgrew the 500-square-foot manufacturing facility. With great enthusiasm, they moved into a new building that had 5,000 square feet. All areas of operations, from manufacturing to sales to collection, were hitting on all cylinders. Things were greater than ever, until an unexpected event called the Great Depression landed on their shoulders. Once again, their fair dealings with customers, employees and suppliers paid off. Because of support from these groups and their unpopular, but necessary, cut backs, survival through these turbulent times was achieved.

In 1935, an incident occurred that catapulted the brothers into national and then international prominence. It was also responsible for the changing of the name of the company to WEMBLEY. The incident was as follows: Sam and Emanuel were still single men living the good life. Emanuel had a love for fine clothing and treated himself to a very expensive new suit. Even though a good suit at that time could be purchased for five to six dollars, Emanuel splurged and paid twenty-five dollars for a beautiful brown suit made of a new fabric called Nor East. It looked like silk, but was made of worsted mohair material. He was proud as a peacock when he showed it to Sam. Sam was most impressed with not only the looks, but the softness of the new material. Emanuel hung the coat on the coat rack and went to work in the factory. As though it were a magnet, Sam could not take his eyes or his hands off the new coat. After making a number of trips to the coat rack to feel the material, Sam noticed that even though he crumpled the fabric on several occasions when he went back it would be perfectly smooth and wrinkle free. It was like nothing Sam had ever seen in a piece of material. It was truly magical. Sam knew that when a tie was worn all day, the wrinkles were there to stay. A tie's life was short lived - possibly five or six wearings was the most you could get out of one. Should he or shouldn't he, was the question running through Sam's brain. The gears of creativity were churning full speed. "What the hey, I'll go for broke." Sam took the coat into the factory without Emanuel's knowledge. He laid it out and cut the pattern of a tie out of the back of the new coat. It took four pieces, as the coat wasn't large or long enough to get a regular cut tie. Sam gave the pieces to the

ladies on the assembly line and swore them to secrecy. They were instructed to give the tie back to him, and him only. At the end of the work day when Emanuel looked for his coat, it was gone. Sam, with a lump in his throat, suggested someone might have taken it by mistake, as the coat rack was by the front door. Emanuel took the loss as just one of those unfortunate things. He hoped that someone would bring it back when he realized his mistake. Sam stuck the tie in his coat pocket. When he got home, he took the crumpled tie out and tied it around his neck. He wore it the rest of the evening. When he took it off to go to bed, he tied a knot in it again. The next morning, he could not wait to untie the knot and smooth it out. He had breakfast, and when he got back, whammo, there were no wrinkles. A smile was generated from ear to ear upon seeing this miracle of miracles. That morning when Emanuel picked Sam up to take him to work, Sam was wearing the tie. Sam did not say anything, hoping that Emanuel would see it. Sam couldn't wait, he squirmed in his seat, it was just killing him to show it to Emanuel, which he finally did. Sam explained the circumstances of what had transpired. Emanuel was overwhelmed by the possibilities of what his brother had discovered, never mentioning a word about the loss of his new coat. Emanuel's reaction was, "The fabric is amazing, it is incredible! It is a miracle." Never an unkind word of the dastardly deed his brother had perpetrated.

They decided that Sam would go to New York and try to get exclusive rights from B. Priestley & Company who made this miracle fabric. The first man contacted was not interested in selling the material for ties. Sam's super salesmanship would not take no from him. The man had to calm Sam down, for Sam was excited to the point of almost having a heart attack. It was lucky for Sam that thirty minutes into his sales pitch, a Mr. Horace Speight, head of the company from the home office in England, came in. Sam gave this gentleman his super pitch on how this product would revolutionize the tie industry throughout the world. Sam told Mr. Speight how much material (on an exclusive basis for tie manufacturing) he would like to order. It amounted to twelve thousand dollars. Sam was advised that if he produced a letter of credit from his bank, the order would be filled including the exclusivity clause. Sam produced the letter of credit and Mr. Speight held up his end of the bargain.

With the new miracle tie, priced at one dollar, they sold, in one week, all they could manufacture in three months. Once again that old menace, cash flow, was ready to reappear. To keep momentum going and to capture the market, $62,000 of material was needed to fill projected orders. The bank said they could not extend a line of credit of that amount unless the company raised an additional $25,000 of capital.

Although full of optimism, Sam and Emanuel knew this

would be no easy task. Money was still hard to come by, and venture capital was practically unheard of, due to economic conditions. As the old saying goes, where there is a will, there is a way. In two days, with the help of some of their influential customers, the $25,000 was raised. The charter of the company had to be changed to include the five new partners (the partnership lasted from 1936 to 1944). In the eight years the partners were involved, they supported the company 100% on everything Sam and Emanuel proposed. One of the decisions made at this time was to change the name of the company. The Nor East fabric was expected to completely

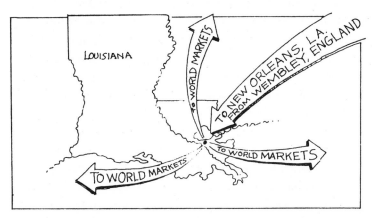

change the course of history of the company. They also realized that, if anything happened to either of the brothers, the company would not have the same personality or profile. The new name selected was, WEMBLEY. This name was chosen for the following reasons: One of the mills producing the Nor East fabric was located in Wembley, England. The other reason, Wembley was a nice-sounding, uncomplicated name. The new name of the company from that day forward would be WEMBLEY.

In 1968, Emanuel's stock was purchased by his brother's heirs. WEMCO, the new name selected for the company, is currently producing thirty-five thousand ties a day. It is the largest tie manufacturer in the world.

MEN'S TIES
ORIGIN

Today, men all over the world wear ties as a fashion statement. Like many other fashion trends, ties came about by way of the military.

In the 15th century, Croatian soldiers (from Croatia, a part of what is now Yugoslavia), being highly superstitious, wore a sort of muslin wrap around their necks, believing this would protect them from their enemies during battle. Apparently, they were taking no chances, for they also wore amulets on chains around their necks as double protection. Amulets, although made of material such as stone, coral, jade, paper, etc., all served the same purpose. They served as a charm to the wearer. Chances are, but no historical proof is available, they also carried rabbits' feet and four-leaf clovers on their persons as well.

In 1636, necks of male citizens of Paris were adorned with many frills and ornamental collars, but not with ties.

This was to change soon when a regiment of Croatian soldiers were garrisoned in the fashion-conscious city. The Frenchmen took to the new fad, which they renamed "Cravat" in honor of the Croatian soldiers who introduced it to

their country. In 1638, two years after the Croatians arrived in Paris, Louis XIV, the fashion-conscious "Sun King", liked the cravat to the point that he made it mandatory to be part of the uniforms of all French soldiers and sailors. Like everything Louis XIV did, it was first-class, as all cravats worn by his military personnel were made of silk. His top regiment, made up of the creme de la creme, was known as the "Regiment of Royal Cravattes".

The cravat didn't take long to make its way into the political arena. The powerful French republicans wore enormous, highly-colored cravats to designate their political affiliations. Soon there were over 100 different types of knots used to tie the cravats. Fashion-conscious men of Paris, wishing to keep up with the fashion trends, were required to take a 16-hour course on the proper tying of this new neck wear.

This new creation originally worn by the Croatian soldiers spread around the world, in modified forms. Styles shifted constantly. In 1692, a French army battalion at a battlefield called Steinkirk was surprised in the early morning hours by the English. There wasn't time to tie the intricate cravat knot. On the other hand, it was unthinkable and unwise to rush into battle completely unadorned. To rectify the dilemma, they simply twisted the strands of the cravats together and tucked them into their button holes. The French won the day, and the new style cravat, daubed "The Steinkirk", swept the continent.

By the last part of the nineteenth century, several new novelties had made their appearances. They were the bow tie, ascot, string tie and the four-in-hand. The four-in-hand soon swept the field and became the uncontested champion of neck wear around the world.

The term four-in-hand referred to the knot used by the

driver to tie the reins of a team of four horses.

In 1930, the fashionable Duke of Windsor, who later became King Edward VIII of England and then abdicated, introduced a shirt with widespread collar points. To fill the area between the points, the Duke invented

the triangular knot that bears his name, "The Windsor Knot". Since 1930, it has been the most popular knot found in ties

around the world. It can be found in either a single or double Windsor depending on the wearer's preference.

BATTLE OF NEW ORLEANS
ODDITIES AND LITTLE-KNOWN FACTS

The Battle of New Orleans was not fought in New Orleans, but in St. Bernard Parish.

A few days before the major battle, General Andrew

Jackson received word by courier that the city council was considering surrender. Jackson's reply was, "If they attempt to convene, blow up the meeting hall."

Andrew Jackson, a short time before the great Battle of New Orleans, ordered release of Jean Lafitte's men who had been incarcerated by Louisiana Governor William C. C. Claiborne. He gave them their freedom with the agreement they would join him in fighting the invading British army. The decision, even though most unpopular with Claiborne, proved to be advantageous to Jackson's efforts. With this agreement, Lafitte supplied the much-needed ammunition to fight the battle. The outcome of the battle would have been different had Lafitte not supplied the ammunition. It was not until two weeks after the battle was over that the government-issued ammunition arrived. The reason: the contract to deliver the ammunition was given to the lowest bidder.

On December 18, 1814, Jackson held a full-dress parade in Place d'Armes. It was to demonstrate a sense of power to calm the nerves of the locals. It proved to do more than that. At the parade, Jackson was amazed at the multitude of different uniforms worn by the military units in New Orleans. He recorded that bit of information in his memory bank. Later, he put it to good use when he found out where the location of the battle would be. On December 22nd, he was advised the British were making camp at Chalmette. He needed more time to prepare. He knew there was no fortification, plus his instructions to blockade the canals in the area were not carried out. His brilliant move was to attack the British army during the night. When the battle was over, a large number of Americans were captured. The British surmised by the number of different uniforms that the city was fortified and well-manned. The decision was made not to attack New Orleans until General Packenham arrived.

After the battle, the British general also wrote a formal protest to Jackson stating fighting at night was barbaric and not a gentlemanly way of war. Jackson responded in so many words saying, "May the bird of paradise fly up your nose."

At the December 22nd night battle, 24 Americans were killed, 115 wounded and 74 missing. That was almost double the number of Americans killed later at the famous battle of January 8, 1815.

Another brilliant military strategy implemented by Jackson was his breaking the levees and flooding the battle area. Even though the British had superior firepower, they had no footing for the big siege guns, and, therefore, no accuracy.

BRITISH MISCALCULATIONS GREAT HELP IN AMERICAN VICTORY

General Packenham also had his well-thought-out plan of attack. His plan called for the firing of rockets to put fear into the Americans. He also planned on attacking from both sides of the river, simultaneously. He unfortunately miscalculated the swift current of the Mississippi River. The barges that were intended to carry his troops to the west bank were swept many miles downriver. By the time the troops on the west bank reached the spot they were to start their attack, the battle on the east bank was long over.

The British troops wore their full-dress parade uniforms. The pure white crossings on the bright red uniforms made excellent targets for the American sharpshooters. The rockets that were supposed to put fear into the Americans apparently only helped their adrenaline flow, for the battle proved to be a massacre. It was said by one of the Kentucky long riflemen, "It was like shooting fish in a barrel."

The Battle of New Orleans was the first major battle where U.S. soldiers from many states stood shoulder to shoulder to fight a common enemy.

It was reported by a journalist that it was true the U.S. gained its independence on July 4, 1776, but that independence was not confirmed until the overwhelming victory at the Battle of New Orleans.

The greatest irony of the famous January 8, 1815, Battle of New Orleans was the fact the War of 1812 was officially over December 24, 1814, the day before Packenham arrived.

JACKSON DAY RACE

"I will smash them, so help me God!"

This was not the vengeful boast of a madman goaded to fury by surprise and the knowledge that he had somehow been betrayed. It was the calculated though swift decision of a battle-minded veteran who knew that one countered suprise with surprise, and that the best defense was often to attack.

Then, in a voice more self-composed, Jackson calmly told his aides: "Gentlemen, the British are below. We must fight them tonight."

He was not prepared for such immediate action. Neither were the troops, many of them only just arrived after taxing marches, many others green and not yet fully disciplined. But Jackson was not a man of caution; nor was this a time for caution. He felt certain that the troops at Villere's, whatever their numbers, could be no more than the British vanguard, and that reinforcements must be on their way. He could not afford to wait.

At 1:55 that afternoon the signal gun at Fort St. Charles

resounded in alarm, scattering the pigeons in the Place d'Armes, bringing anxious housewives to their windows, and alerting the troops around the city that their time, to their surprised delight, had come. Seconds later, the bells of the Cathedral tolled in answer to the triple cannon blast. Couriers sped from Royal Street, west, north and east, to summon the outlying troops to Fort St. Charles and thence to the Montreuil plantation three miles above Macarty's.

Down from Avart's came Coffee's and Carroll's Tennesseans, fumbling with their powder-horns and buckling their belts. They were quickly passed by Hind's Dragoons, trailing clouds of dust as they galloped through the city. From Bayou St. John came Plauche's Orleans Volunteers, running all the way as if they meant to keep on running till they met the enemy. The two regiments of Regulars poured out of the barracks, to be joined by Jugeat's Choctaws and Daquin's Battalion of Free Colored, trotting to the beat of Jordan Noble's drum.

The Commanding General watched them arrive and pass down the Esplanade on their way to Montreuil's. They were a motley crew, their officers shouting commands in French and English, but he found them strangely reassuring. There was not a dragging foot among the lot.

Jackson hastily moved his field headquarters to Macarty's, a two-story mansion with double balconies, now vacated by its ailing owner. From there, overlooking Chalmette's and de la Ronde's, he had a distant view of the British bivouac at Villere's. How many were there? It was hard for him to tell, even with the enemy's fires plainly visible.

The Americans had one asset which the British were without, and would, in fact, remain without, and that was cavalry for reconnaissance. Jackson sent Colonel Hayne with twenty of Hind's Dragoons to scout the British position and report. After a brief encounter with Travers' outpost, in which one horse was killed, two men were wounded and the enemy was alerted, the Dragoons took shelter at de la Ronde's. Hayne boldly rode as close as he dared to the British lines, and calmly studied the invaders through his glass. He returned to Macarty's with the extraordinary information that there were "only two or three hundred" British on the field.

Fortunately, Major Latour, ever scurrying about like a beaver seeking a weak point in the dam, had made his own close-quarter survey of the enemy encampment. He came back with the far more accurate estimate of their numbers - betwween sixteen and eighteen hundred. And what did Jackson have to throw against them? In his report to the Secretary of War he appraised his forces as "not exceeding in all fifteen hundred." He seems to have been overly conservative. Other sources, including the generally reliable Latour, set the figure closer to two thousand.

Jackson was still not certain that the British landing at Villere's was not a feint, screening a second landing at the Chef Menteur. Having recalled Daquin's blacks from the Plain of Gentilly, he now dispatched the Louisiana militia under Claiborne to that post. They would be supported by a detachment of Carroll's Tennesseeans, with the rest of Carroll's men remaining in the city as reserves.

Characteristically, Claiborne complained bitterly of this assignment. He told Colonel Bartholomew Shaumburg, his aide-de-camp, that "this was part of a system decided on to keep me in the background." Shaumburg did not agree. He held with Jackson that the pass should be strongly guarded, since the enemy approach below the city might be simply a diversion. Somewhat mollified, Claiborne began to think that he might be a hero yet, if Jackson's fears of a second landing should be realized.

At McCarty's, Jackson consulted Patterson as to what the Commodore could do with his two vessels on the river. The larger Louisiana, though armed and partially manned with impressed seamen, was not fully ready yet for action. In what physical state was the Carolina? Under the command of Captain John Henley she had recently been fitted with stronger fire power, five six-pound guns on either side and two long-range twelves on bow and stern. Her crew of ninety was disciplined and skilled.

It was agreed that Patterson would board the Carolina, taking Livingston with him as an observer well acquainted with the river's landmarks. The ship would move downstream to a position opposite the British camp. At precisely seven thirty she would open fire, softening up the enemy with a sustained bombardment. Half an hour later, successive red, white and blue rockets would be Jackson's signal to attack.

Towards dusk, Jackson watched the Carolina weigh anchor and start her downstream drift, sails slack, for there was little wind and she rode on the strength of the current. Then Jackson led his assorted army, with the two pieces of field artillery, down the field to the avenue of oaks that stretched from de la Ronde's manor to the river. Here they waited; their movement in the darkness had been undetected.

BEST KEPT SECRET IN NEW ORLEANS
JACKSON BARRACKS-WORTH A VISIT

Do not let the word barracks dampen your enthusiasm for visiting this historic spot with your entire family, for there

is something there for eveyone to see and enjoy.

In 1835, when construction was completed, the name given the fort was New Orleans Barracks. The $185,000 facility, designed much in the manner of an Indian fort, was renamed Jackson Barracks on July 7, 1866, in honor of Andrew Jackson, President of the United States and savior of the City of New Orleans.

Although part of the original construction has been lost because of the erosion of the river, 16 of the original plantation style brick structures, fronted by galleries with Doric columns, are in excellent condition. The buildings are the largest number of antebellum structures assembled in a small area in the entire South.

As you stroll the meticulously manicured quadrangle with magnificent moss-draped trees, you will get the feeling you are back in the 19th century. Some of the men of stature who were stationed at the barracks were Robert E. Lee, Ulysses S. Grant, Pierre Gustave Toutant (P. G. T.) Beauregard, George B. McClellan and John J. "Black Jack" Pershing.

The father of Dwight D. Eisenhower was stationed at

Jackson Barracks, and it was during his tour of duty that he attended a Mardi Gras ball and fell in love with the lady who was to become his wife and mother of a future President of the United States.

Adults as well as children are in for a treat, for the powder magazine which was built in 1837 for the barracks has been converted into one of the finest military museums in the United States. The museum is unique, for it is a hands-on museum where youngsters not only see but are encouraged to touch as well. Outside the museum are large pieces of military hardware, such as tanks, personnel carriers, howitzers, airplanes, etc., that children (of all ages) are invited to climb on and fantasize to their hearts' delight.

Yes, there is something for everyone - grandma, grandpa, mother, father and children - and would you believe, it's all free.

ST. JOSEPH'S CHURCH
SECOND-LARGEST CHURCH IN THE UNITED STATES WHEN BUILT

In 1844, the City of New Orleans had a fast-growing Irish population in the area of Tulane and South Claiborne Avenues. St. Joseph's Church parish was established by the first Catholic Archbishop of New Orleans, Reverend Antoine Blanc. A modest little parish church named St. Joseph's was built on Tulane Avenue across from present site of Charity Hospital.

In 1858, the parish was entrusted to the Vincentian Fathers, who built one school for boys and one for girls. The parish grew rapidly, and, in 1866, a full square of ground in the 1800 block of Tulane was purchased for a new church.

The first order of business: collect needed funds for a building that was to be so large, it would require one million bricks just for the foundation. It would be the second-largest church building in the United States.

Easter Sunday, May 9, 1869, was set for ground-breaking ceremonies. The colorful ceremonies were started in the old church building, and then a parade of all parish organizations with their colorful banners in front, followed by 500 boys and girls all dressed immaculately in white.

Ceremonies at the site, where an immense crowd gathered, were started by Reverend Jeremiah Moynihan, who praised the good Irish people. This was followed by a most unusual ground-breaking ceremony. Irishman Hugh McManus, driving two supposedly Irish mules, plowed the

entire plot of 115 feet by 231 feet, where the church would stand, as thousands of spectators applauded.

October 8, 1871, was set for the laying of the two cornerstones, which was also unusual, and called for another celebration. An impressive platform was erected and a seat of honor was installed for the archbishop. There was a giant yellow banner with large green Gaelic words, Cead Mhille Failte, which meant, "a hundred thousand welcomes".

Into two large copper boxes, one for each cornerstone, were placed a parchment listing all parishoners who pledged financial support for construction and upkeep of the structure, newspapers of the day, coins, church documents and numerous other articles, which were sealed by the archbishop with a beautiful silver trowel.

The architect who designed the church was pleased, for his children served as models for the

cherubs that are at the base of the columns in front of the great structure. He was also displeased because the original height of 200 feet had to be reduced to 150 feet, and both steeples shown on the original plan had to be left off because the foundation would not support the great weight of the structure. From 1875 to 1884, work had to be stopped completely, because of lack of funds and until a contractor could solve the problem of uneven settling, which he did by solidifying the existing foundation.

Sunday, December 18, 1892, twenty-six years after the project was born, the church, although still without pews, stained glass and many other items, including permanent front steps, was officially dedicated. Even though it was the second-largest church in the United States when completed, there was no way the estimated 4,000 who showed up for the ceremonies could be accommodated inside.

ST. JOSEPH'S CHURCH

Location 1802 Tulane Avenue.
Architect: T. C. Keeley.
Architecture is Romanesque.
Builder: D. M. Foley, Jr.
Thomas O'Neil
Interior of the Church-100 feet by 200 feet - 95 feet from ground to roof.
Seating capacity-1600-1800.
1866 Land Purchase.
1869, May 9, ground breaking.

1871, October 8, cornerstones laid.

1875-1884, work stopped because of defects in foundation.
1892, December 18, day of dedication.
1892, December 25, first mass celebrated at 4 p.m., after which

at intervals of 1/2 hour, low masses were held up to 10 o'clock.

THE AVENUE
OF
CHURCHES AND SYNAGOGUES

Because of its striking beauty and colorful history, we sometimes overlook the fact that St. Charles Avenue (originally Nyades Avenue) is also the avenue of ten churches, two synagogues and two private homes that were previously churches. With this many places of worship, it is apropos that the avenue has a saint's name.

The tallest of the religious structures, located directly across from Audubon Park, is Holy Name church, which is part of Loyola University. It has, in addition to its height, breathtaking beauty and history. The church organ pipes were originally the organ pipes used at the 1884 New Orleans World's Fair.

Beautiful Rayne Memorial United Methodist Church is located on the corner of St. Charles Avenue and General Taylor Street. The gothic revival building is completely different in architectural style from Holy Name. It has a unique history all its own. The church was erected in 1875 with the first services celebrated January 2, 1876. The original name, St. Charles Avenue Methodist Church, was changed to its present name in 1887 in honor of Robert W. Rayne, a New Orleans merchant who paid for more than half the cost of construction. He did so in honor of his son, who was killed in the Civil War.

A plaque over the door of the church reads "To Him who redeemed me and hath kept me all my life-and in memory of my son William who was fatally wounded at Chancellorsville."

For many years, the tall and delicate steeple of the church has been illuminated at night, giving the church the name "The Church of the Lighted Steeple".

When one lives on the avenue, finding a place of worship, no matter what your religious convictions, is as easy as catching a trolley, and no doubt more stimulating and uplifting.

SAD TIME IN CITY

In July, 1763, the year after Louisiana's ownership was passed from France to Spain, another passing, or more de-

scriptive word, "expelling", took place. The city's first land owners, the proud Jesuit Fathers, were expelled from Louisiana. They were also expelled from all French as well as Spanish-owned lands.

Their property, which extended from present-day Canal Street to approximately Jackson Avenue and from the river to beyond Claiborne Avenue, was confiscated and sold by the king.

Of course, and no doubt with the inspirational and spiritual help of their founder, Ignatius Loyola, they prevailed and later returned to Louisiana. When they did, they were more dedicated to their ideals than before.

New Orleans, without the influence and good work of these good men who labored for the Society of Jesus, would in no way be the great city that it is today.

As they say, you can't keep a good man down. In this case, they didn't keep the good Jesuits down for long. On August 7, 1814, the Society of Jesus was restored by Pope Pius VII.

IMMACULATE CONCEPTION

The Jesuit church in the 100 block of Baronne Street was constructed in the Arabian architectural style.

The Russian dome is made of iron and is 35 feet above the roof.

The Russian dome was put into the design of the church as a sign of the Jesuits' appreciation for Catherine the Great's efforts on behalf of the order during its troubled times.

Many of the Jesuit churches throughout the world have the architectural style of many nations to show their appreciation to those who were sympathetic to their cause.

CITY'S OLDEST CHURCH BUILDING

The oldest church building in New Orleans is our Lady of Guadalupe Church on North Rampart and Conti. This famous old church was built in 1826 and was, upon completion, called "The Mortuary Chapel".

In the 1870's, due to the large number of Italian immigrants living in the area, the church was rededicated as the church for the Italians and renamed "St. Anthony of Padua Church".

A bold sign, Parrocchia Italiana, was painted across the entire facade of the building.

GALLATIN STREET
HELL ON EARTH

There are today two short blocks in the French Quarter called French Market Place. The location is directly behind the U.S. Mint and runs from Barracks to Ursuline Street. Nearby, truck farmers have fruit stands, and a flea market is held on weekends. Before the area was known as French Market Place, the two blocks were known as Gallatin Street.

In the nineteenth century, these two blocks near the New Orleans riverfront were considered the roughest two blocks in the world. Some claimed they were more notorious than the entire Barbary Coast. It had taken a great deal of effort to gain the reputation as the most noted cesspool of immorality, flagrant wickedness and crime on the face of the earth. A writer, after visiting Gallatin Street, gave the following description.

It is likened to Sodom and Gomorrah of old. The harlots of Gallatin Street, and the proprietors who owned them, established new lows to which human beings might sink. Every known human vice was indulged in, with the exception of gambling; on Gallatin Street it was not necessary to gamble to get the clientele's money. When the prostitutes and the bars concluded their fleecing, if a man left Gallatin Street with any money in his pockets at all it was considered a miracle. Even the Police Force of the City of New Orleans refused to go into Gallatin Street day or night, no matter how many men were available; Gallatin Street had its own law, as bad as it was.

From dawn to dusk the street was deserted, as if its occupants were vampires who slept while the sun was out to be rested for the shadows of night.

GALLATIN STREET
WICKEDEST-FILTHIEST-BAWDIEST

No one in his right mind ever went to Gallatin Street alone day or night. Even parties in a group were putting their lives on the line. A wealthy young

Creole named Parmalee made the mistake of going there with a group of friends while he was slightly intoxicated. He was never seen again. His prominent family did everything possible to find out what happened to him. Only by chance, a year later, did the family learn that the prostitute who had collared him in one of the dancing halls had hocked the ring she had stolen from him that night. And on her death bed she told the story of how he, along with a group of other young men, were shanghaied and sold to the captain of the sailing ship Eberhard. Newspaper accounts of the Eberhard indicate the ship sank off the coast of Norway several months after leaving the Port of New Orleans. All hands were lost.

BIG

When most people think of New Orleans, they do not necessarily think "big". Natives, for the most part, don't think of it in that realm either. This is really not a correct assumption based on the following information.

In the 1884 New Orleans World's Fair Handbook, New Orleans is listed as the largest city in the world in land area. It is pointed out to have been eight square miles larger than the second-largest city, London, England. Many other cities incorporated land adjacent to them through the years, and eventually, numerous cities surpassed New Orleans in size.

The main building of the fair, covering 33 acres, was the largest building, until this day, ever built for a world's fair. The building had an auditorium for entertainment, and 18,000 people could be accommodated with no obstructions in viewing the stage. To fill the spacious hall with music, the largest organ ever constructed was built, installed and utilized for the entire duration of the fair.

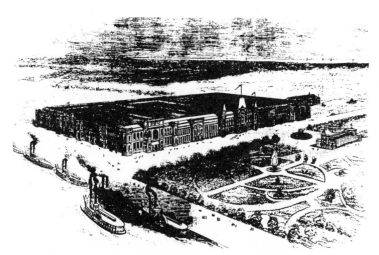

Today, the city has the largest tract of undeveloped land (New Orleans East) of any major city in the country.

Jazz was not only born in this city, but the annual New Orleans Jazz and Heritage Festival is larger than the next three jazz festivals combined.

At the end of the 19th century, the largest privately owned monument was built in Metairie Cemetery. The monument is the final resting place of Mr. and Mrs. Moriarty.

The federal government undoubtedly had big expectations of New Orleans. Prior to the Civil War, they began construction of the U.S. Customhouse. When completed, it was the largest building owned by the federal government.

With necessity being the mother of invention, New

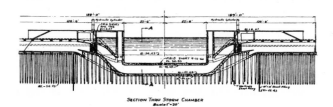

SECTION THRU STORM CHAMBER
Scale 1"=20'

Orleanian engineer Albert Baldwin Wood designed, built and installed the largest drainage pumps in the world. He also designed and supervised construction of the largest drainage system in the country. At 14 feet in diameter, the pumps are big enough for an 18-wheeler to run through when the impellers are removed. In a city predominantly below sea level, coupled with almost 60 inches of rain per year, the pumps were a welcome addition to the water-soaked city. Someone jokingly said we either had to find a way for collecting and disposing of the water or we would have to grow gills. Another of the city's world's big records is also one of the city's best kept secrets. This is because of the old adage "Out of sight, out of mind". In addition to having the largest drainage pumps in the world, the city also boasts of having the largest syphon in existence. It, too, is used in the city's unique

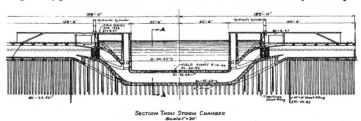

SECTION THRU STORM CHAMBER
Scale: 1"=20'

system for collecting and disposing of rain water. The never-seen (underground) piece of equipment is used to move rain water collected on the west side of the Industrial Canal. From there, it is sucked by the syphon under the Industrial Canal to the east side where it continues its flow to Lake Borgne by way of a series of pumps. The syphon is 10 feet below the bottom of the canal and measures 45-1/2 feet wide by 10 feet high and is approximately 200 feet long. The syphon is truly an engineering marvel. If a survey were taken amongst the average citizens, chances are only a handful of people know that such a device even exists in the city.

To the east of the canal, you will find the present-day Martin Marietta facility. When built during World War II, it

was the largest building in the world under one roof. The structure was used to assemble military equipment needed to fight the war. Today, Martin Marietta builds the external tanks used to launch NASA's space shuttles. The workers are justifiably proud, for there has never been a delay in the lift off of the space shuttle caused by a failure of the largest component of the space shuttle system built by Martin Marietta. The external tanks measure 28 feet in diameter by 154 feet long. It is not only the largest component, it is the only component of the space shuttle system that is not re-used.

Gambling has been big since the very founding of the city. Right after the Civil War, New Orleans could boast of having the biggest lottery in the world. The Louisiana lottery operated daily, weekly and monthly drawings. The top prize

for the monthly drawing in the 1800's was the unbelievable
sum of $600,000. Just think, this was in the days when the
winners were not taxed. In the near future, the city will be
the home of the second-largest gambling casino in the U.S.
Or as they now call it, "gaming" facility. The casino will be
located at the foot of Canal Street close to the river.

With New Orleans having the oldest Mardi Gras in the
country, it is not surprising that some records are held in this
area. Our Mardi Gras is called the biggest free show on earth.
It also boasts of having the biggest Mardi Gras float. The
Endymion Krewe has a tandem float that is 130 feet long and
carries 140 masked riders. The Elks Krewe of Orleanians
truck parade that follows the Rex parade is the largest parade
in the country. It has had as many as 175 decorated 40-foot
long trailer trucks with an estimated 50 riders per truck. All
are masked and throw bushels of goodies to the frantic public. Before moving from the parade category, New Orleans
holds the record for the largest float ever used in a parade.
The float was used in the ceremonies for the dedication of the
Henry Clay statue on April 12, 1860. The popular statue was
located on the Canal Street neutral ground between St. Charles

Street on the American side and Royal Street on the French Quarter side. A three-mast, 50-ton sailing vessel was taken from the river, placed on a massive undercarriage and pulled down Canal Street by mules. It went around the statue and was then returned to the river and refloated.

New Orleans being big on food, again it is only natural that she scored in this area. During the Southeast Culinary Association convention held in the city in 1995, the largest muffaletta ever conceived by man was made, consumed and thoroughly enjoyed. It measured approximately 3-1/2 feet thick by 7-1/2 feet in diameter. The thirst generated by that monster could have emptied the water from a small swimming pool. To guarantee continued excellence in food, the largest cooking school in the world is held each year with approximately 1,000 students in attendance each day. The city's greatest chefs donate their time and share their expertise, with all profits generated going to St. Michael's School for Exceptional Children.

Even though City Park is not the biggest municipal park in the U.S., it does hold the record of having the largest number of ancient oak trees in the country. The New Orleans Glass Works holds the title of largest in its field in the U.S. Wemco is the largest manufacturer of men's ties in the world. Of course, without saying, the Louisiana Superdome is the largest domed building in the world.

Last, but not least, it has been reported, and unanimously agreed upon, that New Orleans politicians have the biggest egos without any group coming remotely close to catching up with them in this auspicious area.

I hope that after reading this big article, your outlook of the city is bigger than before.

REALLY BIG
LOUISIANA SUPERDOME

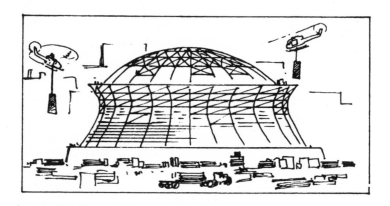

It may have been controversial, but it has certainly been a plus in the economy of the area.

When first proposed, the residents of Louisiana were allowed to vote on whether they were for or against the project. The cost was estimated at 35 million dollars. In 1966, the majority voted "yes". When the world's largest domed building was completed in 1975, the estimated 35 million had ballooned to an estimated 168 million. Chances are, we will never know what the final cost really was. One thing we do know, the building of the Louisiana Superdome has been labeled as "one of the wisest decisions any city or state has ever made". It was, without question, the catalyst for the changes that first spread throughout the central business district, and then to every nook and cranny of the city's businesses.

Dave Dixon is rightfully called the "Father of the Louisiana Superdome". He is a man of vision, as well as a man of action. Knowing the importance of timing, he waited for the opportune time to move his massive and, yes, controversial proposal to the forefront. There were many opponents to his idea, saying it was too grandiose. Of course, a project this size involved politics. Doesn't everything? Vic Schiro, close to the end of the campaign while running for mayor, had the misfortune of being hospitalized. The appendix operation he had may have been considered minor, but the results were major. It was a most critical time in the election. Like vultures, his opposition seized the opportunity. They seemed to be saturating the media, both electronic and print, with Vic flat on his back and not being able to fight back. His being confined to a hospital bed was like a ship floating listlessly in the water.

Dave Dixon, knowing that every stumbling block is also a stepping stone if you have a positive attitude, saw this as his golden opportunity. Dave approached Vic with his Superdome concept and suggested he call a news conference right there in his hospital room. The mere size and controversy of the proposal would surely captivate the attention of the media. Governor John McKeithen was made aware of the project and agreed it was a good one, joining the team. The outcome was a win, win, win situation. Vic was elected mayor. The Superdome became a reality, and the city of New Orleans

was the recipient of the largest domed building in the world.

There is a lesson to be learned in this story. The next time misfortune crosses your path, why not sit down and look at it in a positive way and see how you can turn things around, like Dave Dixon helped Vic Schiro turn his misfortune into good fortune for not only himself, but the entire city.

INTERESTING SUPERDOME FACTS

Construction began August 11, 1971.
Building opened August 3, 1975.
Total land area (building, garages and grounds) 52 acres.
Height 283 feet.
Roof 9.7 acres.
Structural steel 20,000 tons.
Air conditioning 9,000 tons.
Parking in garage 5,000 cars and 250 buses.
Electric wiring 400 miles.
Note: the Astrodome would comfortably fit inside the Louisiana Superdome with space to spare.

REALLY, REALLY BIG
WORLD RECORD

This is another story reference the possible origin of the term "What a revolting development this is!"

It may be true that practice makes perfect, but Mrs. Joseph Sinatra, the mother of 10, and, therefore, an experienced deliverer of babies, was not remotely ready for what was to transpire when delivering her 11th bundle of joy on December 15, 1914. It turned out the baby was more than a bundle of joy. This little dude, weighing in at 22 pounds when he saw the light of day for the first time, was given the rightful nickname "The Little Man". One would think that immediately after being slapped on the bottom and clearing his windpipe his first request was for an oyster po-boy dressed and a slice of apple pie, followed by a glass of cold milk to wash it down.

No doubt sensing a record, midwife Mrs. Stella Guth Reynolds of Algiers, who handled the delivery, called for not one but two scales. The Little Man was placed in each, and an accurate weighing was done on both scales to verify his official weight. Ev-

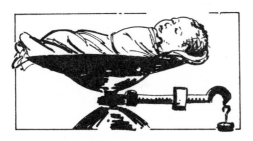

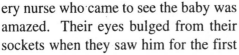

ery nurse who came to see the baby was amazed. Their eyes bulged from their sockets when they saw him for the first time. At 22 pounds, it was a world record. As would be expected, his huge size was followed by his all-consuming appetite. Several days after he was born, he was weighed again. This time the scales showed 26 pounds.

The baby was normal in every respect, with the exception of his weight. With the average newborn weighing in at 7 pounds, he was more than three times the average. He was lucky, for his father owned and operated a grocery store at 1433 Patterson Street in Algiers. The first problem that was encountered after his birth, thank God, was not medical. Nevertheless it had to be overcome. None of the hand-me-down baby clothes from the eight living brothers and sisters were large enough for him. Alterations were made without delay.

This world record made the Sinatra's home a beehive of activities for a long long time. People from all parts of the city, state and nation came to see The Little Man.

It is not unusual when people see babies for the first time they are apt to mention what beautiful eyes they have. In this instance, after delivering her 22-pound baby, many, when seeing Mrs. Sinatra, no doubt said "My, what big eyes you have."

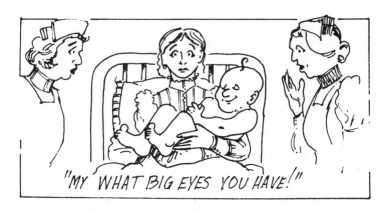

"MY WHAT BIG EYES YOU HAVE!"

PROCRASTINATION AT ITS BEST

"Never put off until tomorrow what you can do today" is not now or has ever been the motto of our political leaders. The following story, you will no doubt agree, bears this out.

John McDonogh, a highly successful businessman, owned large tracts of land on both sides of the Mississippi

River throughout the State of Louisiana. Every year when the snows melted, causing the river level to rise, McDonogh's pressure rose along with it. He knew from previous experience rising waters would and could top the levees or break them. Either way, both brought destruction to property and crops and took great quantities of money from his coffers. McDonogh was also a philanthropist. He did not mind giving his hard-earned money to needy causes, but he did not cotton to the rampaging river being the cause of his loss of funds.

McDonogh learned again from experience that the river frequently broke the levee above New Orleans at the Bonnet

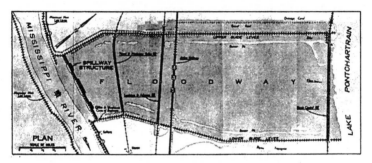

Carre' (meaning square bonnet) Plantation. When it did, the water proceeded into Lake Pontchartrain in making its way to the Gulf of Mexico (see map showing seven courses of the river). Studies showed the river was trying to go back to one of its previous routes of thousands of years ago.

McDonogh also knew he needed political backing to achieve his goal of controlling the river. In 1829, he went head to head with the political leaders to accept his proposal of a man-made spillway at the site of the Bonnet Carre' Plantation. The project was studied. In fact, like many other sound proposals, it was studied to death. When McDonogh died

October 26, 1850, his zeal for pushing the spillway project through the legislature also died. Finally, in 1927, the greatest national disaster ever suffered by the people of the United States occurred when the river went on a rampage. In some locations, the river became many miles wide. Hundreds of thousands of people were displaced, and many lives as well as crops were lost. It took this great disaster to serve as a wake-up call for the federal government. Curtailing the continuing losses caused by the rampaging river was finally set as a priority. The Corps of Engineers was given the task of mastering the mighty serpent called the Mississippi River. For too long, the river moved at will like a slivering snake down the central part of the United States. Because it was the main artery of commerce and the number one waterway in North America, the government's number one priority became finding ways of controlling Old Man River. The McDonogh proposal from 1824 was dusted off and, finally, over 100 years later, the project became a reality. The Bonnet Carre' Spillway was finished in 1931.

There was no doubt McDonogh knew how to make money. He also knew what he was talking about way back in 1824 reference the river. Since its dedication over 100 years after McDonogh proposed it, the spillway has done what he said it would do. Each time it has been opened, rising waters have been successfully diverted to the Gulf of Mexico by way of Lake Pontchartrain. This reduced the volume of water and the height of the river as it passed the highly populated area of New Orleans.

EIFFEL TOWER

Paris, France was the site of the World's Fair in 1878. The main attraction and the only permanent structure was the

 Eiffel Tower. At 984 feet, it was the tallest man-made structure in the world, surpassing the height of The Great Pyramid in Egypt built 5,000 years earlier by the Pharaoh Cheops. For many years, there was a restaurant near the top of the tower. It offered a magnificent view of Paris available in no other way, with the exception of hot air balloons.

After many years of wear and tear, an engineering study recommended the restaurant, because of its weight, be removed for the structural integrity and safety of the building.

Upon learning of the restaurant's proposed removal, a New Orleans entrepreneur was successful in purchasing and bringing it to New Orleans. Each part was painstakingly marked prior to dismantling. Its pieces were crated, shipped, and upon arrival, like a giant jigsaw puzzle, reassembled at 2040 St. Charles Avenue. When opened, it was appropriately named the Eiffel Tower.

Today, the structure is owned and operated by the Pontchartrain Hotel. It is used for weddings, banquets and other social and business events.

ANOTHER EIFFEL TOWER TIDBIT

With France being predominantly Catholic, the 1878 World's Fair began with celebration of the Holy Sacrifice of the mass held directly under the structure. It was most fitting, for the tower seemed to reach for the heavens. A beautiful altar was built and installed specifically for the occasion.

After the fair, a Catholic couple from Convent, Louisiana, who attended the mass at the opening ceremony and were impressed with the beautiful altar, returned when the fair closed. They went with the express purpose of purchasing

the altar and transporting it to their hometown. Upon its arrival, it was installed in St. Michael's Church, and for over 100 years it has been used to celebrate the Holy Sacrifice of the Catholic mass.

NEW ORLEANS
HUEY P. LONG BRIDGE

From the very beginning, the mighty Mississippi River has been an economic asset to the city. The main reason New Orleans was founded where it is is the river. From the very beginning, the number one rung on the city's economic ladder has been the river.

As they say, nothing has ever been perfect; the river is no exception. With the arrival of railroads, the problem of crossing the river became a huge obstacle. To overcome the watery barrier, railroad ferries were built to carry the cars across so they could continue on their journeys. Before this means of convenience became obsolete, there were five different crossings. The largest went from the area of Audubon Park to the Westwego property now occupied by Avondale Shipyards.

In 1930, a river bridge study was made for the City of New Orleans, and the recommendation was accepted. Construction of a train bridge to cross the river began. During construction, Governor Huey Long decided it would be in the best interest of the state for the bridge to also carry motor vehicles. He was, without question, a man of vision. He knew that in order to remain competitive with more and more trucks on the highways, more roads and bridges would have to be built. He approached the project with the same fervor he approached everything else. He advised that if a roadway was added to each side of the bridge, the state would pay half the cost of construction (now you know why the roadways are so narrow-only so much additional weight could be added). He also very slyly slipped in the suggestion that the bridge would be more recognizable if it carried his name.

When completed, it made the port of New Orleans more competitive. The increased tonnage handled allowed the port to grow and expand. With it, the city's prosperity also grew.

Huey always thought big. Possibly the reason he made such a sweet deal with the City of New Orleans in construction of the bridge is that he learned the train bridge, being 4-1/2 miles long when completed, would be the longest such bridge in the world. It holds that title until this day.

It may seem a little strange, but the facts are the city is the only one in the country that owns a railroad (Public Belt Railroad) which operates more outside of the city than within. It also owns and maintains a train bridge outside of the city, as well as an airport (New Orleans International) that is also outside of the city limits.

AUDUBON PARK NATATORIUM

To be cool and to cool off in the hot summers before the days of air conditioning, all one needed to do was to go to the

Audubon Park swimming pool. To little children, it looked as big as Lake Pontchartrain. One small child who went for the first time was overheard asking his father, "How many miles long is this thing, Daddy?"

The pool was opened on May 3, 1928. On May 16, Hollywood's Tarzan, Johnny Weismuller, exhibited the skills that made him a world champion swimmer.

The humongous, double-sided pool that could accommodate over 1,000 customers offered more than swimming. Directly in the center was a water fountain. It sprayed water high into the air and out the sides. As the water fell, it broke down into a mist that was most cooling on a hot, humid summer day. I often wondered if the person who invented the fine mist machine used to cool NFL players on the sideline at games played in the warmer weather cities had the same fond memories of the Audubon Park pool fountain and used that pleasant experience to come up with the NFL sideline cooling mist machine.

For those who mustered the courage to climb the stairs to the high diving board, not only did they get a bird's eye view of the pool and surroundings, they also had the exhilarating experience of diving head first (almost all small children jumped a number of times to get the courage to dive head first). Before hitting the water, their hearts and stomachs felt like both were in their throats. If that was not exhilarating enough, at the same time you wondered if you were going to hit the concrete bottom or not.

Through the years, other enjoyable attractions were added. One summer, a long, colorful serpent was the attraction. Possibly the people responsible for operating the pool had made a trip to see or read about the infamous Loch Ness monster.

Another enjoyable addition to the fun was the building of an 80-foot by 150-foot sand beach on the uptown side of

the pool. Where else could you go and sunbathe on a beach right in the heart of the city? To keep the sand from getting into the pool and causing damage to the pumps, showers were installed along both sides of the covered walkway that connected the beach and the pool.

Those responsible for operating the pool were very imaginative in finding ways to have the pool provide multiple areas of entertainment. Each year when the pool was

emptied for repairs and painting, time was set aside before painting so that the children could go skating in the bottom of the same pool they swam in.

Yes, they skated around and around in the bottom of the pool on both sides of the 75-meter paralleled sections to music from huge speakers attached to a juke box.

The enjoyment of those who attended kept entire families coming back again and again. The pool was financially self-sustaining, plus, at times, generating a sizable profit. One year, it was so successful, the $125,000 profits were used to purchase land adjacent to the park for baseball fields.

In closing, one could say, if, as a child you never went to look cool at the pool and to be cool, you were a fool.

NEW ORLEANS'
TEN GREATEST NEWS STORIES

The ten news stories listed below are considered by a panel of local historians as the most important historical events in the city's history.

A quick look reveals an overabundance of drama-packed tragedy-laden events.

(1) Occupation of the city by federal troops in spring of 1862.

(2) The Battle of New Orleans January 8, 1815.

(3) The lynching of eleven Italians on March 14, 1891, after the city's police chief had been ambushed and murdered by the mafia assassins.

(4) The so-called White League Battle on September 4, 1874, at the foot of Canal Street, when white citizens wrested control of the city from Carpetbagger-Republican clique that had ruled during Reconstruction.

(5) Hurricane Betsy September 9, 1965.

(6) The great Yellow Fever Epidemic of 1853.

(7) The consummation of Louisiana Purchase on December 20, 1803.

(8) The destructive Good Friday fire of March 21, 1788.

(9) The slaying of five leaders of the French settlers by the Spanish governor on September 28, 1769.

(10) August 1988 National Republican Convention.

The writer has taken the liberty of selecting #10, based on the fact that the approximately 20,000 members of the TV, radio and print media did more to promote New Orleans during this event than the coverage of any other single event in the city's history, or the combined coverage of the last Super Bowl, Final Four and Mardi Gras.

NOTE: Items that make the news today have results which are no different than those of the past. Of the ten news stories listed, only two had a positive effect on the city -- The Louisiana Transfer and the GOP convention. The remaining eight were all destructive in one way or another -- wars, fire, flood, hurricane, disease, lynching and insurrection.

**NEW ORLEANS SAVED TWICE
ONCE FROM BRITISH ARMY
ONCE FROM MIGHTY MISSISSIPPI
BOTH TIMES IN THE SAME GENERAL
LOCATION**

In 1927, one of the greatest national disasters in the history of the United States occurred. Heavy snows the previous winter, coupled with unusually heavy rainfall, caused the mighty Mississippi River to reach a height never before recorded. Flooding up and down the Mississippi River rendered 700,000 people homeless, with over $200 million in damages. In Louisiana alone, 1,300,000 acres of prime farmland were under water.

New Orleans, a city located in an area below sea level, was most fortunate. Local meteorologist Issac Monroe Kline, after studying his calculations, advised city fathers that unless the levees were raised New Orleans would suffer a major flood. The city heeded his warning, using sandbags to raise the height of the levees. Even with the increased levee height, a small amount of water still lapped over the top. As the old adage goes, if anything else can go wrong, it usually will --

and did. On April 15, 1927, New Orleans recorded its heaviest rainfall in history; in a 24-hour period, the city received 14.94 inches of rain. The coup de grace was the New Orleans Public Service losing all electric power. Helter-skelter was everywhere. An emergency meeting was called. After a long conference between the state and city authorities, plus the U.S. Army Corp of Engineers, it was agreed that the desperate situation in New Orleans required drastic actions. It was feared that the levee would fail from the pressure exerted by the rain and weakened levee conditions. If this happened, there was a threat that, of the 600,000 people who lived in New Orleans, tens of thousands would likely drown. It was decided that an artificial crevasse (man-made break in the levee) would have to be made below New Orleans to reduce the anticipated level of the flood waters. The logical location decided upon by those in charge was at CAERNARVON (13.7 miles below New Orleans), which is located in a sharp bend in the river between the Poydras and Orange Grove Plantations.

On April 25th, a large crowd gathered on the levee at Caernarvon. Their numbers included engineers, government

officials, reporters, and some very irate people whose homes and land would soon be under water. In a sense, they were the sacrificial lambs who were to be offered up to save the people of New Orleans. The people of Caernarvon and the surrounding area were as mad as hornets whose nest had been disturbed. They shouted in unison, "Let nature take its course and choose her own victims." In response, they were told not to worry, they would all be reimbursed for their losses. This did about as much good calming their anxieties as putting a bandaid on a gunshot wound.

Without delay, divers were sent into the muddy waters to strategically place, well below the water line, 15,000 pounds of dynamite. When all was ready, the crowd was warned to get back and cover their ears to protect themselves from the expected deafening roar of the explosion and the rushing flood waters. There was some embarrassment when the demolition superintendent set off the charge and only a soft, muffled sound was heard, and only enough damage was caused to allow a small trickle through a very small opening. Over the next two days, divers placed additional tons of dynamite. As each charge was set off, engineers were surprised at just how strong the levee was. One said, "It is almost as difficult to destroy them as it was to build them." After numerous attempts, the crevasse finally opened to 2,600 feet. The waters flowed out of the river into Breton Sound. As expected, the water level at New Orleans was reduced. Unexpected was the extreme hostile reaction of those whose homes were sac-

rificed. Retaliation was expected from the group of home owners on the levee that had little by little been transformed into a mob. The National Guard had to be called out. Soldiers with rifles and machine-guns were stationed up and down the levees both above New Orleans and within the city limits, to be sure that none of the threats to blow-up the New Orleans levees were carried out.

The one good thing that did come out of the great flood of 1927 was the government's passage of an act in 1928 marking the end of serious flooding to the lower Mississippi Valley.

The Bonnet Carre' Spillway was built, and, when necessary, has been successfully used to divert 250,000 cubic feet of water per second from the Mississippi River into Lake Pontchartrain.

It is interesting to note that John McDonogh, one of the largest landowners in Louisiana, in the first half of the 1800's proposed that a spillway be built at the site of the Bonnet Carre' Plantation, the exact location where the government built the Bonnet Carre' Spillway almost 100 years later.

GENERAL PACKENHAM
A BLUE, BLUE CHRISTMAS

Christmas, traditionally a day of happiness and good cheer for hundreds of millions of Christians around the world, proved to be a time of doom and gloom in 1814 for British General Sir Edward M. Packenham, Commander of the British forces sent to take the City of New Orleans. Upon arriving at the site where the famous battle would take place, selected by the Admiral of the Fleet before Packenham arrived, the general was virtually in shock. He was literally between the proverbial rock and a hard place. The land was flat and soggy, plus the field was extremely narrow. Although there were seven possible areas to attack the City of New Orleans, with six almost assuring victory for the British, the Admiral selected the seventh site (some historians feel because of animosities between the two men), where the Americans had more than a chance for victory. To back out once the site had been selected would be tantamount to losing face. It just wasn't done by gentlemen who made their living at warfare. Packenham just had to do the best with what he had, which wasn't much. On his right flank was an impassable, useless swamp that served as a hiding place for the menacing Indians. On Packenham's left flank was the Mississippi River with its swift current and a steamboat outfitted with cannons that could move up and down the river, making for a difficult target, with the ability to fire at will on his unprotected flank. Across the river, also trained on his unprotected troops, was a battery of cannons. To his front, was a water-filled moat backed by a sturdy rampart. Behind the rampart, although ragged looking, were expert cannoneers and riflemen from various states throughout the country. To make matters worse, as if conditions could be any worse, the General's supplies were 35 miles to his rear, over almost impassable terrain.

No doubt, after surveying the situation, the first act performed by General Packenham on this cold, miserable, rainy

AFTER LOOKING OVER THE SITUATION PACKENHAM WRITES HIS WILL.

Christmas Day in 1814 was to sit down and write his last will and testament.

On January 8, 1815, at the now famous (in the eyes of all Americans) Battle of New Orleans, the inevitable happened. His troops were being slaughtered like fish in a rain barrel. They began to retreat en masse. In a last-ditch attempt to rally his men, Packenham led the last charge he would ever make. He was shot and killed. As was customary for the time for a fallen commanding general, his heart was removed from his body and buried on the field where he fought so valiantly. His remains were then placed in a barrel of rum (to preserve the body) and shipped back to England.

COUNTIES OR PARISHES?

In December of 1803, the United States received formal possession of the vast lands of the Louisiana Purchase. After the official transfer, Congress divided the Purchase into two parts. The lower part, comprised of approximately the present State of Louisiana, was called the Territory of Orleans and was governed by a legislative council. The vast upper portion was called the District of Louisiana.

Political controversy began almost immediately when the Territory of Orleans was divided into counties, just as all other existing states were divided. They were listed as Acadia, Attakapas, Concordia, German Coast, Iberville, Lafourche, Natchitoches, Opelousas, Orleans, Ouachita, Pointe Coupee and Rapides.

From 1682 until 1803, Louisiana was owned, controlled and, for the most part, occupied totally by two Catholic countries, France and Spain, who did not have rules and regulations stressing a separation of church and state. To the contrary, the church and state were one.

The population of the Territory of Orleans was small and scattered. The few roads that did exist were very poor, and, in most areas, there were no roads. After mass, parishioners would gather outside the church for religious news, announcements, and instructions. Church parishes were the hubs of most activities for the populace. For this reason, those who lived in Louisiana did not want and would not accept the term "county". It was bad enough that overnight they found themselves becoming American citizens. True, they were now American citizens, but they would not give up those things to which they were accustomed without a fight.

In the second session of the 1807 legislature, before Louisiana received statehood, an act was passed which provided for the subdivision of the Orleans territory into 19 parishes, but it did not abolish the original 12 counties. The 19 parishes were Orleans, St. Bernard, Plaquemines, St. John, Ascension, Lafourche, Interior Lafourche, Iberville, Baton Rouge, Pointe Coupee, Concordia, Ouachita, Rapides, Avoyelles, Natchitoches, St. Landry, and Attakapas, or St. Martin.

These political subdivisions were derived to make each existing church parish the focal point of each subdivision. This was done, without a doubt, to soothe some of the ruffled feathers.

On February 16, 1811, President Monroe approved an act of Congress that enabled the people of the Territory of Orleans to call a convention for the purpose of adopting a constitution and state government for admission into the Union. Congress prescribed that up to sixty constitutional representatives should be appointed among the counties, districts and parishes of the Territory of Orleans. The legislature of the Orleans territory declared there would be 45 representatives -- all from the original 12 counties and not from the 19 parishes.

On January 22, 1812, the constitution of the State of Louisiana was finally drafted, adopted and signed. Each delegate signed for the county from which he was elected. The constitution did not specify or subdivide the state into counties or parishes. Theory: let the sleeping dog lie. In the second session of the legislature, the state was divided into seven judicial districts by parishes. From that time on, the word "parish" superseded "county".

In 1816, William Darby published his parish map of Louisiana. He intentionally left out the county divisional lines. He felt this would be too confusing. Did this lead to the final death of the term county? No. Lo and behold! The act of December 16, 1824, provided the sheriff of the Parish of St. John the Baptist to be an ex-officio sheriff of the County of German Coast. The controversial subject of the term "county" was back in the political picture once again. It was mentioned as German Coast County as late as March 27, 1842.

The Louisiana Act of February 29, 1844, separated the state into six electoral districts for presidential electors. They were separated by counties.

Finally, after the 40-odd years of subdivision confusion, the 1845 Louisiana Constitution superseded the state constitution that originated the county system in Louisiana. The word county did not appear a single time in the new constitution and was finally laid to rest.

NOTE: Of the present 64 parishes, some are divided by water (example: parts of Orleans and Jefferson Parishes are on both sides of the Mississippi River). Only one parish is divided by land. St. Martin has Iberia Parish sandwiched in between the two sections of St. Martin Parish.

FIRST ELECTRIC OUTDOOR SIGN

The first electric sign in the city of New Orleans was on the Arlington Annex Building located at Basin and Iberville Streets.

It was such an oddity, on opening night prior to the lighting of the sign, the area looked like Mardi Gras with people surrounding the building as far as the eye could see.

The main building, when constructed, had a 30-foot-long mahogany bar that was the largest in the country when installed.

On opening night, the newspaper reported it was a thing to marvel at. Besides the horde of locals, hundreds of people who represented the big breweries and wine companies from all over the country were in attendance as well. More than 100 cases of champagne were sold, patrons outbidding each other for their favorite vintages. Before the night was over, everyone was walking in champagne.

The main attraction at the Anderson Annex was not the building, but Tom Anderson himself. Anderson was a state representative of the Fourth Ward in New Orleans for many years. Although he was the owner, in all the years that he was in the saloon business, Tom Anderson never mixed or served a drink himself.

Through the years, Tom Anderson's annex was the meeting place of famous people from all over the world, from John

L. Sullivan, world champion heavyweight boxer, to Babe Ruth and Ty Cobb of baseball fame. The list of luminaries stretched from political leaders to socialites to actors. It was stated that the list of famous people, if written down in very small print one below the other, still couldn't fit on the 30-foot-long bar.

REMINDER OF THE PAST

To the east and west of the old Pontchartrain Beach area on Lakeshore Boulevard, you will find two 30' tall, faded, red and white steel poles. One pole stands approximately 150' in front of the other. One pole has a square on top, and the other one has a circle. These poles were bright red and white in color when installed in the early 1940's. They were erected for the purpose of clocking the speed of PT-boats built in New Orleans by Higgins Shipbuilding and Higgins Marine. PT stands for patrol-torpedo, since these craft carried out patrol duties and carried torpedos for combat.

Prior to World War II, Higgins had manufactured commercial and pleasure boats. During the early part of the war, Andrew Higgins received a government contract to construct landing craft and PT-boats. Andrew Higgins was very innovative and is credited with being the inventor of propelling torpedos by air compression as opposed to the then-familiar use of gun powder which would create smoke and thereby compromise the position of American craft.

Both Higgins shipyards worked around the clock seven days a week. They completed seven landing craft every day, and one PT- boat every seven days. The landing craft were later used in the invasion of Normandy. Once construction of the PT-boats was completed, the vessels were loaded onto trailer trucks and taken to the Industrial Canal plant where they were outfitted for the Navy. After they were inspected, they were filled with fuel and readied for testing in Lake Pontchartrain. The tests were conducted by timing the vessel between the two pairs of poles, which were set one nautical mile apart.

Each PT-boat was equipped with four high-speed Packard engines of about 2500 HP each. The boats were highly maneuverable, with speeds of 50 knots (or 57 miles) per hour.

After almost 50 years, the poles, although dull in color and rusty, are still there in case those pleasure boat owners who want to test their speed can do so between the one mile nautical markings left from World War II.

SUNDAY
OPEN FOR BUSINESS NOT NEW

The following is taken from writer John Williamson Crary, Sr.'s memoirs entitled, "Reminiscences of the Old South From 1834 to 1866."

"My first impressions of its peculiarities seemed to me like a sudden transfer to some strange foreign city. It was on Saturday about the last week in January, 1835, that we arrived at the flatboat landing of New Orleans. Next morning after late breakfast, I concluded to walk out and see my first quiet Lord's day of rest in a Louisiana city. As soon as I got out in a street I saw the drays, wagons and carts going and coming in every direction. As I proceeded I saw the stores open and the people in their business garbs and habits seemed to be using the most extraordinary energy and anxiety. I said to my companion, "We have lost a day, this must be Monday."

"No," he replied, "this is the day for everything and everybody in New Orleans."

As I proceeded down old Levee Street, the gambling and liquor saloons were all open and in full blast. The steamboats were discharging and receiving cargoes, the drays were hauling cotton, sugar and upper country produce, the markets were all open and full of people, the military companies were parading the streets. The whole scene was unique, grotesque and profane. It was neither a gala day nor a carnival, but a heterogeneous composition of all that human tongue, action and motive could inspire for selfish and material gratification. The desecration of the Sabbath was never a crime in New Orleans and, until the Northern and Southern people of the old states took the lead, which was about 1850, Monday looked more like the Lord's day than Sunday."

As the old saying goes, history does have a way of repeating itself.

AIRPORT
SHUSHAN-NEW ORLEANS

Current government regulations specify that municipal buildings cannot be named for anyone still living.

A prime example of the wisdom of this decision is

pointed out in the following story.

At approximately the same time the State Capitol Building in Baton Rouge was conceived and ramrodded through the legislature by Huey Long, a new airport for New Orleans was also in the works. It was to be named "Shushan Airport" for one of Huey's staunch supporters. The same quality construction materials, expensive embellishments and luxurious furnishings were used in both structures. The airport literally reeked with grandeur and the name of Shushan. Brass door knobs, brass plaques and massive monograms in the terrazo floors expounded the name Shushan. The facility was officially opened February 9, 1934. City, state and national political and business leaders were in attendance. Some of those at the dedication ceremonies mentioned that it looked as though the building was a shrine to Mr. Abe Shushan. His name appeared to be just everywhere space would allow.

During the governorship of Richard Webster Leche, 1936-1939, the darkest political cloud of suspicion ever to hang over Louisiana, other than the Reconstruction era, was about to open up and wreak havoc on those who were doing misdeeds in the political arena. Along with Governor Leche, 149 political leaders and businessmen statewide, including Shushan, were indicted. Of those, 49 were found guilty in what was labeled "Louisiana Scandals". One of the men indicted and found guilty along with Governor Leche was LSU President James Monroe Smith. He was sentenced to 30 years at the state penitentiary at Angola. Leche was found guilty of a long list of offenses, including diverting federal funds from the Works Progress Administration (WPA) for his private use. Leche received a 10-year sentence at the federal penitentiary in Atlanta. One of Leche's more memorable quotes was "I swore to uphold the Constitution of Louisiana and the United

States, but I did not take any vows of poverty."

Having been found guilty and sentenced, the name Shushan had to be removed from all facets of the building. It was said to have cost a great deal more to remove the name and replace it with other materials than it did for the original installation.

The name of the former Shushan Airport was changed to New Orleans Lakefront Airport.

Yet another controversy stemmed from the construction of the airport. Enrique Alvarez's nude figures in the pool in front of the airport created a tizzy. Nudity in the 1930's was

not as acceptable as it is today. The controversial statues led to an ongoing confrontation between the art world and everyday citizens. One art lover, in defense of the statues that exposed all, claimed they inexplicitly represented the exposing of the crimes of those who went to jail.

BREAD

Bread baked in New Orleans is one of those food items that visitors marvel over. And New Orleans' people, while taking it for granted, consume it in enormous quantities. I personally believe the two best inventions of all time were French bread and stretch pants. With the latter, you can eat all of the former you want.

It is interesting to note that New Orleans consumes more French bread than any other city in the world, including Paris, France. It is ironic that, although there were over 400 bakeries in New Orleans as little as 50 years ago, almost all of the French bread baked in New Orleans today is baked by only four concerns -- two German and two Italian bakeries. Curiously, there are no longer any Frenchmen baking French bread in this fair city by the river.

An amusing story was told to me by a man who many old timers claim was the "greatest of the great" when it came to baking French bread. He was the late Leopold J. Sandbrink. The good German was owner of Sandbrink Bakery, located at 940 Desire Street and founded in 1883. As a young man working for his father, Gerhard, one of Leopold's jobs was to supervise the personnel responsible for treating the water to make the bread the following day. This was before the advent of water purification plants, so all water consumed had to be treated by those who used it.

The employee whose job it was to "clarify" the water became ill and sent his son in his place. Advising Sandbrink that his father had given him all necessary instructions, he said he was ready to go to work. Going to the river, he filled the barrels, returned and treated the water "as instructed by his father". The next day, the water was used, and the bread was delivered to regular customers from house to house. Before finishing his deliveries, Sandbrink was hailed by some very unhappy patrons who insisted he taste the bread. When he did, his mouth drew up tightly, and he immediately thought of the new man settling the water.  Calmly he went back to the bakery and asked the replacement to show him how he had done the job. The black man said, "just as my poppa told me: one bucket of coal and one bucket of alum." Sandbrink was flabbergasted! The process called for one bucket of coal and one small scoop of alum (about 50 times less than a bucket). The young man begged for mercy, pleading that he not be fired, "or poppa will kill me." Sandbrink, still not excited, said he would not fire him, but to help him remember what happened when too much alum was used to settle the water, made him eat one whole loaf of the bread. As Mr. Sandbrink told me, "You know, he never made that mistake again." Which may prove that there is a lot to be said for first-hand experience.

CHAPTER TWO

FLAGS

INTRODUCTION

Flags representing countries can be traced back in history for thousands of years. The armies of the Roman Legions carried flags and banners long before the time of Christ -- the Bible makes references in two separate places to a type of flag or banner.

June 14th is the date Americans celebrate Flag Day across the nation, for it was on June 14, 1777, that the first description of the American Flag appeared in the journals of the Continental Congress. It stated "The flag of the United States will have 13 alternating red and white stripes, let the Union be 13 stars, white in a blue field representing a new constellation".

This chapter covers all of the flags that have flown over Louisiana since its founding. They include city, state, national and special event flags. Also covered will be the little-known display procedures and their use in celebration during bridge construction.

FIRST AMERICAN FLAG TO FLY OVER THE CRESCENT CITY

December 20, 1803, was a very special day in the city's history. It was on that day Louisiana was officially transferred from France to the United States. Place d'Armes, present-day Jackson Square, was a beehive of activities. Mixed emotions were evident during the removal of the French flag and raising of the American flag. Creoles, whose hearts and allegiance were totally dedicated to France and Spain, were very sad. On the other hand, the equally proud Americans were jubilant.

With pomp and ceremony, the French flag was lowered very slowly down the flag pole. Tradition dictated that, when removed, it was to be firmly wrapped around the senior French naval officer. With a contingent of armed sailors, the officer and flag were escorted to and taken on board a French vessel. The ceremony up to this point was rather somber and silent. When the American flag was raised, Americans jubilantly voiced their approval. The loud cheer was cut short when the American flag stuck for a short time while ascending the pole. It was almost an omen of the Europeans' wish that the ceremony not be completed.

FIRST AMERICAN FLAG FLOWN WAS DIFFERENT!

The first American flag to fly over the city was different. True, it was red, white and blue with stars and stripes. The difference: the American flag flown on that auspicious date had 15 stars and 15 stripes. The thinking up until that time was a new star and a new stripe would be added for each

of the new states as they joined the Union. The Louisiana Purchase added so much territory, a decision was quickly made reference the flag's design. The original 13 states would be represented by 13 stripes. As new states entered the Union, a star would be added in the blue background of the flag.

CITY FLAG

The official flag of the city of New Orleans was adopted on February 6, 1918. It is white with edgings of blue and red with three fleurs de lis grouped in triangular arrangements on the white field.

The flag design was selected from 379 entries in a contest during the city's 200th anniversary year (1918). The field of white represents purity of government. The blue is for liberty, and the red represents fraternity. The stripes symbolize democracy. The fleur de lis was chosen from association with the French royal arms.

During early years of exploration, the French explorers carried the flag of fleur de lis to the New World and to Louisiana. The fleur de lis is representative of the birth and infancy of New Orleans and is a symbol of the city's French heritage.

OFFICIAL MARDI GRAS FLAG

On Mardi Gras and during the Carnival season, you will see many, many Mardi Gras flags. Many are used for indoor and outdoor decorations. A smaller number is proudly displayed on flagstaffs.

The official flag can be easily distinguished from the unofficial flags. On the vast majority of Mardi Gras flags, you see the purple, green and gold tricolors running straight up and down the length of the flag. The official flag, made only for those who serve as king or queen, has the tricolors running on an angle to the length of the flag. On the official flag, gold is always in the center flanked by the green and purple. The reason: The crown of the king or queen is located in the center gold section. If the flag is for a king, it will have a purple crown. For the queen, the crown is green. If a husband and wife serve as king and queen of the same krewe, and this has happened in the past, the purple crown goes on one side and the green on the other.

The official Mardi Gras colors, purple, green and gold, came about because of the first Rex costume in 1872. It consisted of a purple robe with green rhinestones and a scepter and crown of gold.

The most-asked question of Mardi Gras is, "What do the colors stand for?" The 1892 Rex parade theme was symbolism of colors. According to the king of Mardi Gras, purple represents justice, green is for faith, and gold is for power.

GREATER NEW ORLEANS BRIDGE

On your next trip to the Westbank by way of the upriver span of the Crescent City Connection, might I suggest you look up as you approach the superstructure? In doing so, you will see a large metal plaque depicting a flag with a pelican and four white stars. The flag represents Neville Levy's appointment as an admiral in the shipless Louisiana navy.

More importantly, it serves as a reminder to all, had it

not been for Captain Levy, the bridge that is indispensable to the thousands who use it daily would not have become a reality for many more years, if ever. He began his efforts for a much-needed bridge in 1950 and did not renege on his commitment until the bridge became a reality. When countless others threw monumental obstacles in his path, the Captain, as champion of the bridge, didn't throw in the towel. Instead, he simply worked harder, persisted and persevered. During all of his years and countless hours that he spent on the project, he never expected or received any financial gain. His only wish was that one day the bridge would be named in his honor. When completed in 1974, the bridge seemed destined to bear his name. The Chamber of Commerce, Board of Trade, International Trade Mart and other influential business groups backed resolutions calling for the naming of the bridge the "Levy Bridge". Unfortunately, all efforts fell to naught. The bridge was called the Greater New Orleans Bridge.

When the new twin-span bridge opened on September 30, 1988, some people felt calling the bridges the Greater New Orleans numbers one and two seemed too much to bear. Republican State Senator Fritz Windhorst, from Harvey, announced a contest (for school children), sponsored by the local newspaper, to name the old and new bridges. Contest rules stipulated that the spans could not be named for anyone living or dead. With this rule, there was no possibility of the bridge ever being named for the man who championed it from start to finish. The winning entry was the Crescent City Connection.

The only reminders of Neville Levy's tireless efforts in making the bridge a reality are the navy blue (flag) plaques at each end of the original span.

Even though Mr. Levy never received proper recognition for what he achieved, he did fare far better than Joan of Arc, the young French maiden who single-handedly was responsible for saving Orleans, France, from the British Army. For her efforts she was classified a heretic and burned at the stake.

Although not as drastic as Joan's treatment for her efforts, it seems being acknowledged Admiral of the shipless Louisiana navy, although not physically cruel, could be considered equally as cruel as Joan's fate.

HISTORY

Louisiana has the distinction of having had more different flags fly over its territory than any of the other 49 states. Of the ten different flags, eight have flown over New Orleans during its colorful history. The two that did not are the British flag and the flag of the free and independent Republic of West Florida.

THE TEN FLAGS OF LOUISIANA
EXPLORATION OF A NEW WORLD

In 1519, the Spanish explorer, Alonso Alvarez de Pineda, led an expedition along the northern shores of the Gulf of Mexico. He reported discovering the mouth of a great river - in all likelihood, the mighty Mississippi.

THE FRENCH TAKE POSSESSION

The first explorer to travel down the Mississippi River to its mouth was Frenchman Sieur de LaSalle. In 1682, he took possession of "the country known as Louisiana", naming it Louisiana in honor of his king, Louis XIV.  For a century and a half, "Louisiana" referred to a vast area that makes up several of our present-day states.

SPANISH POSSESSION

In a secret treaty in 1762, France ceded its territory west of the Mississippi to Spain. Colonists in Louisiana didn't learn of the transfer for almost two years!

ENTER THE BRITISH

In 1763, Great Britain acquired parts of Louisiana east of the Mississippi from France and Spain in the Peace of Paris that ended the French and Indian War.

RETURNED TO THE FRENCH

The cost of maintaining distant colonies, and worries about restless Americans who wanted to control the land, led Spain to return the Louisi-

ana territory west of the Mississippi to France in another secret treaty in 1800.

INDEPENDENT LOUISIANA

For two months after seceding from the Union in 1861 and before joining the Confederacy, Louisiana flew the flag of an independent nation.

AN INDEPENDENT TERRITORY

The area east of the Mississippi River was still part of Spain's West Florida Territory, but colonists there took control and created their own independent republic in 1810. That same year, that republic joined the United States as part of the Louisiana Territory. People of Louisiana today still refer to the area of the state east of the Mississippi as the Florida Parishes (Louisiana is divided into parishes instead of counties).

LOUISIANA BECOMES A STATE

On April 30, 1812, Louisiana became the 18th state to join the Union. William Charles Cole Claiborne was elected its first governor.

FLAGS OF THE CONFEDERACY

The southern states that seceded from the Union to form the Confederate States of America adopted their first flag on

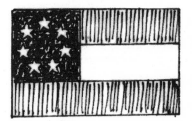 

March 4, 1861. It was called the stars and bars. Because it looked so much like the federal flag, it caused confusion on the battlefield of Bull Run, requiring a second flag to be designed. This one was known as the "Battle Flag" and was ordered by the Confederate Congress. It has become the most recognized of the four Confederate flags. It was white with a union of red and blue saltier bordered in white and charged with 13 white stars. On March 4, 1865, the flag was altered and an upright red band was placed on the flying edge for visibility. This became the fourth and final flag of the Confederacy.

Louisiana's own General P. G. T. Beauregard was one of the designers of the original Confederate flag.

UNION, JUSTICE AND CONFIDENCE

In 1912, the Louisiana State Legislature officially adopted the present state flag. It depicts the

state bird, the eastern brown pelican, and the state motto,
Union, Justice and Confidence.

THREE FLAGS IN TWENTY DAYS

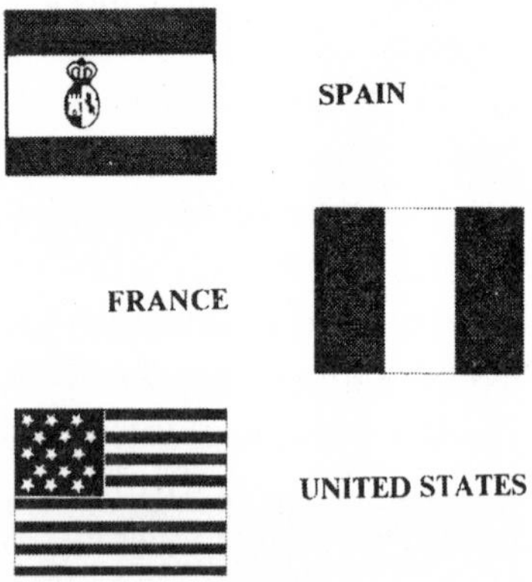

On November 30
1803, Spanish Governo
General Juan Manue
deSalcedo transferred the
Louisiana Territory back to
France after 34 years o
Spanish rule. Napoleon im
mediately turned around
and sold the Louisiana Ter
ritory to the United States.

On December 20th
the official transfer tool
place in the Cabildo in New
Orleans. The transfer became official when American com-
missioners William C. C. Claiborne and General James
Wilkinson took control from French representative Pierre
Clement de Laussat.

In just 20 days, the flags of three different nations officially flew over the city.

THREE FLAGS IN TWENTY DAYS

SPAIN

FRANCE

UNITED STATES

TRADITION

Major bridges are constructed by working from their
anchors at both ends of the bridge simultaneously.

When the final length of steel connecting the two ends
is lifted into place, the American flag is hoisted with the steel.

On January 3, 1958, the final length of steel connecting both ends of the Greater New Orleans Mississippi River Bridge was hoisted into place with the American flag proudly displayed.

ONE OF A KIND

There are numerous regulations to ensure that the American flag is properly manufactured, displayed, stored, etc. There is even a procedure on how to properly dispose of a flag once it is no longer suitable for display.

It was not until this century that a regulation stated how

the stars in the flag were to be placed in the solid blue area.

Jackson Barracks Military Museum has on display an ibly worn, it is proudly displayed at the museum for all to see.

TWO LITTLE KNOWN REGULATIONS

1. There is only one official time when another flag can fly over the American flag. Aboard ship when at sea, the church flag is allowed to fly over the American flag when church services are being conducted.

2. At an event where the head table and speaker's podium are elevated, the American flag is placed to the right of the speaker. If the head table and speaker's podium are

on the same level as the audience, the American flag goes to the right of the audience.

CHAPTER THREE

PICTORIAL-HISTORICAL

INTRODUCTION

As the old saying goes, "A picture is worth a thousand words." With this in mind, the aim of this chapter is twofold.

First, a short, descriptive writing of a multitude of historical anecdotes which I hope you will find interesting, entertaining and educational, augmented with photos, or drawings when pictures are not available.

Second, as you read the written material and absorb the photos on each page, to have you say many times before completing the chapter, "I didn't know that."

SUPER CHARGED CHICKENS

Cockfighting has been a competitive sport for as many years as there has been a Crescent City. Today, it is outlawed, but chances are, if you had a cock and wished to take part in this illegal activity, one would have little or no trouble finding a competitive event.

Through the years, cockfighters have learned special techniques in how to revive their game birds when they looked like they were death warmed over. Between rounds, the trainers would supercharge their warriors by blowing a mist through a straw down the beak of the animal. The supercharged fluid was made of bourbon and finely ground red and black pepper. Once the cock  inhaled this concoction, its eyes would bulge, feathers on its neck would stand erect, and it was once again ready to take on any and all comers.

UNUSUAL JOCKEYS

Marketing of one's products is as old as mankind itself. Like they say, find a different way to entertain, and human curiosity will make them come. History also shows that the more competition, the more creative the juices of entrepreneurs become.

Horse racing in the Crescent City has been active for

over 200 years. Unlike today when there is only one track, at different times in the city's history, there were many tracks in the metropolitan area.

As a new marketing tool, one savvy entrepreneur came up with a novel twist for entertaining the patrons between races. Its success drew patrons to the track like moths to a light.

Just before the main betting event of the evening, grey-hound dogs mounted by monkeys wearing jockey silks raced

to the excitement and delight of the crowd. The race not only turned out large crowds, it also added to the race track's receipts at the end of the day. Patrons were allowed to bet on the unorthodox race, as well as the horse races.

The event proved you can separate a fool from his money, make a monkey out of him, and, at the same time have him enjoy himself.

VISITOR'S NIGHTMARE

Just imagine yourself in a visitor's place in this scenario.

Please keep in mind the visitor's total lacking of any knowledge of the city.

Entering New Orleans by way of I-10 from the east, you exit at Orleans Avenue and head towards the river. In just a few blocks, you notice the street name becomes Basin. You say to yourself, "My, that was strange." Five blocks down the road, you cross Canal Street. When you do so, the street name changes, this time to Elk Place. You no doubt scratch your head in disbelief, only to find out that as you go only two more blocks, you are now on Loyola Avenue. Knowing full well you did not turn, and, therefore, are still on the same street, you pull out a bottle of Excedrin to calm your nerves. Before the pills dissolve, you are seven blocks down the road where you find yourself on Simon Bolivar.

In that short, distracting, hair-raising drive, the same

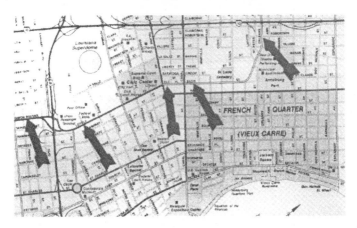

roadway's name has changed four times. To further the confusion, the same roadway was an avenue, street, boulevard and place.

If you think that would be confusing for out-of-towners,

just imagine what they might have thought if they later crossed the intersection of South Carrollton and South Claiborne Avenues. Their heads undoubtedly would have turned 360 degrees, not believing what they saw -- two south streets crossing one another. That could not be. But, in New Orleans, what could not be in other cities is commonplace here.

PIN MONEY

This term comes from the 1800's, when pins were such a luxury it became a custom to give brides money specifically to purchase pins; hence the term "pin money".

BOURBON BOULEVARD?

In 1836, a controversial proposal was presented to the city fathers. The visionary proposer promised to make Bourbon Street the "Broadway" of New Orleans.

In London and many other major cities throughout the world, tearing down buildings to build wide thoroughfares to enhance commerce was the rage. It was believed by the proposer that making Bourbon Street a boulevard, by tearing

down all the houses on the lake side of the street, would increase property values from $500,000 to $750,000. When completed, the street would be 40 feet wide with 15-foot sidewalks on each side.

Even though the Bee Newspaper published a favorable editorial on May 13th, the bold step of altering the fabric and character of the Quarter died for lack of support. The drastic measure was considered detrimental to the Quarter by the majority.

One can only surmise what might have happened had the proposal been implemented. Chances are, not as many people in the U. S. would know the name Bourbon Street as do today. After all, Bourbon Street is where people from all over the world go to "laissez les bon temps rouler".

HEADS UP

In this instance, heads up was a no-no for a sport that was popular prior to the Civil War. To participate, your head had to be down. This unique sporting competition was called head butting. The game (and no doubt the contestants) was very simple. Two male par-ticipants (women were far too bright to ever think of taking part in this odd sport) stood a given distance apart, bent over at the waist. Upon a signal, they ran as fast as they could, hoped for the best and butted heads with their opponent. The contestant left standing was declared the winner. It was reported that large sums of money were wagered on favorite pates.

Without a doubt, this was a sport that required very little

athletic ability and even less common sense.

HERO - HACKETT BRIDGE

If you are not familiar with the Hero-Hackett bridge, don't despair, there is a good reason.

In 1920, yet another attempt was made to span the mighty Mississippi River at New Orleans. Although all other efforts had failed, hopes of reality for the new proposal were high. Confidence may have gone to overconfidence, for, as engineers drew plans, local businessmen pushed the idea hard to reach the point for a permit to be issued. But, in spite of all the effort, that is as far as the project went. Administration leaders changed, plus economic conditions sank to an all time low. It was called The Great Depression. As great as those obstacles were, they were not the real reason the bridge did not become a reality. The main cause of failure was in the

design of the proposed bridge. The bridge had helical roadways on large towers on each end instead of the typical long sloping approaches.

As someone said, the idea was as screwy as the proposed helical roadways.

The Hero-Hackett Bridge was to be named for its designer, Allen S. Hackett, and westbank businessman and chief promoter, George A. Hero.

THE LIBERTY BELL

New Orleans has the double distinction of being:

1. The only city other than Philadelphia to exhibit the Liberty Bell.

2. The only city honored with a second visit.

The Liberty Bell's first visit to New Orleans was for the 1884 World's Fair; it stayed from January 28, 1884, through June 13, 1885.

The second visit was November 19, 1915. Mayor Martin Behrman declared the day a general holiday in appreciation of the distinguished honor conferred upon the citizens of New Orleans.

ELUSIVE LIBERTY BELL

In 1950, six U.S. copper firms financed and had 2,000-pound replicas of the original Liberty Bell cast for each of the states and territories.

That same year the U.S. Treasury Department distributed the bells to all states and territories in support of a savings bond drive.

The Louisiana bell, securely mounted in headstock and frame, arrived in New Orleans with much fanfare and hullabaloo. From New Orleans, it was taken on a six-week tour to twenty-two cities in Louisiana and then placed in the Arsenal Building (part of the Louisiana State Museum complex) in New Orleans.

When the U.S. Bicentennial was nearing, those Orleanians who were familiar with the replica of the Liberty Bell began making plans to use it in their celebration, only to learn the bell had been t r a n s f e r r e d unostentatiously in 1972 to the old Arsenal Museum on the present state capitol grounds in Baton Rouge. As the old saying goes, never two without three.

(1) New Orleans was once the capital of Louisiana-Baton Rouge now holds this distinction.

(2) New Orleans was once the home of the replica of the Liberty Bell-Baton Rouge now holds this distinction.

(3) New Orleans is the home of the Louisiana Superdome-Baton Rouge-?????

RIOT AT NEW ORLEANS' FIRST WORLD'S FAIR

On February 11, 1884, exhibitors at the New Orleans 1884 World's Fair became so disenchanted with the management that 160 of them turned into an angry mob, broke down the exposition entrance gate and held an indignant meeting.

A resolution suggesting that Congress be urged to defeat pending appropriations was threatened. Thanks to several leading exhibitors the threat was never carried out.

Two local newspapers sided with the mob. The Daily Picayune wrote that it did not wish to see the whole business community condemned because of the mismanagement of an enterprise over which it had no control. The Mascot newspaper reported "The bubble had burst, Mardi Gras had come and gone, the days that were to redeem the great shows had passed and a colossal white elephant was floundering in a mire of stupidity, mismanagement and...corruption as helplessly as ever."

Some things seem to never change.

EARLY FLIGHT

On February 6, 1910, French aviator Louis Paulham thrilled a crowd of 30,000 spectators with his fearless climbs, dives, dips and turns high above the City Park race track. These inaugural aerial acrobatics were highly successful and fully responsible for opening the flood gates of flight in the city.

Paulham's airplane was very similar to the one shown in front of the City Park race track grandstands in 1911. If the stands look familiar to New Orleanians, they should. They are the same ones used at the Fairgrounds race track until a fire destroyed them several years ago. At about the same time the race track at City Park closed, the Fairground stands suffered a se-

vere fire December 28, 1918, three days before the opening of its racing season. To remedy the dilemma, the City Park stands were dismantled, put on wheels, and pulled by mules to the Fairgrounds, where they were reassembled.

NEW ORLEANS-ROYAL WEDDING

In one hundred and twenty three years, only one Rex, King of Mardi Gras has married his queen.

In 1895, Frank T. Howard, (one of five members of his family to gain royal honors from Rex) married his queen, Lydia Fairchild.

TV EDITORIALS

He is number one in TV editorials. Who, you ask? Phil

Johnson with Channel 4, of course. Phil has been writing and presenting editorials at the station since 1962. In all of those years, only one other person did an editorial at Channel 4. Actor Sebastian Cabot, who played Mr. French on the popular television show "A Family Affair", presided in Johnson's place. Cabot, who was gloriously bearded, was in town as a guest of the United Way.

Phil wrote a United Way editorial, and, just for fun, let Cabot deliver it. On a couple of other occasions, the courtesy was offered Cabot. Again, he graciously accepted. Cabot would conclude each editorial (all written by Phil Johnson) with the words "And that is good. Of course any resemblance to me by any other editorialist, I can as-

sure you, is not only entirely coincidental, but oftentimes even disconcerting. Good evening."

The last time Cabot played Phil Johnson, he was not a well man. Threat of stroke had taken its toll. It showed on his face during his last TV appearance when he delivered the editorial. Shortly after Cabot completed the editorial, the station got a call from an admirer of Phil Johnson and expressed his concern for Phil and recommended he see a doctor. This, it was learned after a period of time, was not the only TV viewer who thought Phil and his good friend Sebastian Cabot were the same person.

POLITICS OR DUELING, BUT NOT BOTH

In the early 1800's, many political leaders were either seriously wounded or killed in duels. With self interest in mind, and having the power to make laws, they were instru-
mental in outlawing duels and requiring an oath stating that they had not engaged in a duel since the adoption of the state constitution.

With this new requirement, no one could call them cowards, even if they were. As they put it, they were just obeying the law.

FLEUR DE LIS
LIGHT STANDARDS ON CANAL STREET

An old truism we have all heard states: when you live close to the forest, you sometimes don't see the trees. Another old saying is: never ask a native about the history of his city. The reason: he is possibly too close to the forest to see the trees.

Pieces of history about New Orleans that people by the thousands pass every day of the year without paying any attention to are the light standards on Canal Street from the river to North Rampart and down North Rampart to the Municipal Auditorium.

If you look at these very closely, you will note the three large glass light globes are arranged to represent the fleur de

lis, which is the emblem of France. The reason is: they were a gift from the people of Paris, France, to their sister city, New Orleans.

When they were dedicated on February 24, 1930, Canal Street became the most illuminated main thoroughfare in the world.

There is one other interesting piece of trivia reference the light standards: the man who threw the switch to turn on the lights the first time was none other than Thomas Edison.

SPEED REGULATION
BEFORE CARS AND TRUCKS

In the mid-1800's, long before motorcars and trucks were the main means of transportation, Chartres Street was the busiest street in the French Quarter. At times, it became a virtual race track.

To put a harness (excuse the pun) on the excessive speed

of horse-drawn wagons and carriages, the city passed ordinance number 5379CS. The ordinance required drivers to walk their teams on Chartres Street between Canal and Conti. Violators of the ordinance were fined a hefty $25. In the 1800's, $25 would buy a lot of oats, and, no doubt, turned the drivers into slowpokes when driving on Chartres Street.

HELLO BOYS

Alexander Graham Bell invented the immediately popular, indispensable telephone in 1876. In that same year, New Orleans entrepreneur W. H. Bofinger attended a demonstration put on by Bell at his booth at the 1876 Philadelphia World's Fair. He was duly impressed and bought the franchise for Louisiana. He quickly realized the telephone was the communications of the future, and, therefore, wasted no time in having them installed in the Crescent City.

By 1879, the city had 100 subscribers. This was enough to justify the city's first telephone directory, which also has

the distinction of being the second oldest directory in the country.

The first telephone operators were young boys who were quickly dubbed "Hello Boys". In time, they proved to be temperamentally unsuited for the work, and were finally replaced when all deserted their posts when it started to

snow. They could not resist the phenomenon and went outside to play in the snow; they were ultimately thrown out of
work and replaced by more dependable adult females.

ARCHITECTURAL COMBINATION
CLOSE TO PERFECTION

As you drive or walk down beautiful St. Charles Avenue
or through the palatial Garden District, you will immediately
notice that many of the two-story homes have fluted columns.
The columns on the bottom level are topped with Doric-style
decorations, while the second floor columns are topped with
Ionic-style decorations. This same combination of Greek architecture is also found in many famous temples throughout
Greece, including the Parthenon
on the Acropolis in Athens.

The reason for using both architectural styles on the same
building lies in the Greek belief
that wisdom and beauty are a rare,
yet desirable, combination. The
simple Doric architectural style
represents wisdom, and Ionic represents beauty. Hence, the building is blessed with a winning
combination believed by the
Greeks to be close to perfection.

NYDIA UNDER GLASS!

No doubt, the majority of people are as familiar with the
term "pheasant under glass" as they are unfamiliar with the

term "Nydia under glass". Please rest assured, both do exist. The latter came about thusly:

New Orleanian Albert Baldwin Wood was a world-renowned inventor. Locally, he is affectionately labeled the father of the city's highly efficient drainage system. Wood loved his family, his work, the City of New Orleans, and his 28-foot wooden sailing vessel named Nydia. When he died

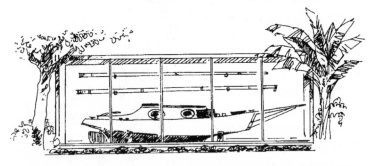

in 1956, he left the city a drier place by providing the largest drainage pumps in the world. With his leadership, the Sewerage & Water Board could boast of having the most efficient drainage system to be found on the face of the earth. His family, prior to and after his death, were more than adequately taken care of. The only thing left was his beloved Nydia. She had given him endless years of enjoyment. In return, he wanted to insure that she would be around and admired for a long time. In his will, he left a vast fortune to his alma mater, Tulane University. There was only one stipulation. Nydia had to be preserved under glass for 99 years. Tulane University graciously accepted the money, and carried out his request by enclosing Nydia in a glass structure on the Tulane campus next to the swimming pool.

According to his will, Nydia will be there through the year 2055, and, without a doubt, for many years after that.

CANAL STREET'S FIRST BUSINESS

Henry Samba was a remarkable free black man who owned a sizeable herd of longhorn cattle. In 1793, he purchased a barn near present-day Canal Street, using the site for his cattle business. He used the Commons (now Canal Street) for grazing his animals.

This was the first business on what later became known as Canal Street.

It is interesting to note - because Canal Street is New Orleans' main street - New Orleans is the only major city in the country without a street named Main.

RENOWNED ARCHITECT
BENJAMIN HENRY B. LATROBE

Latrobe, one of the architects of the White House in Washington, D.C., arrived in New Orleans in 1819. He unfortunately died of yellow fever the following year. Although here for a very short time, he was prolific during that period. His first project was designing the original U.S. Customhouse. It was located on the same site as the current Customhouse, but much smaller. His next project was the Louisiana State Bank building on the downtown lake side of Royal and Conti Streets. Today, the structure houses the Manheim Galleries. Latrobe's last job was designing the city's first waterworks. It was located on Ursuline and Levee Streets near the river. The unique design took water from the river, processed it, then conveyed it to residents throughout the French Quarter through wooden (cypress) water pipes. Unfortunately, he did not live to see the project completed. It did not begin operations until two years after his demise.

The famous architect's remains were buried in St. Louis No. 1 Cemetery. Although renowned, and known to be buried in the ground, today it is not known where in the cemetery his remains were laid to rest. There is a plaque in the rear of the cemetery to commemorate his burial.

The project left undone by Benjamin Latrobe was carried on by his son, John. He, too, is buried in St. Louis No. 1 Cemetery. Yes, the location of his remains within the cemetery is also a mystery.

TO BE TRULY NATIVE!!!

It has been said, with tongue in cheek, that in order to be classified a true native Orleanian, one must have a minimum of one gross of Mardi Gras beads in his attic, a roach sighted on his premises on seven consecutive days, and his

home must have been
flooded at least once.

Anyone having lived
in the city his entire life
without achieving the
above would be more
unique than the LL&E
white alligators with blue
eyes covered in chapter one.

IS CANAL STREET THE WIDEST STREET IN NEW ORLEANS?

ELYSIAN FIELDS AVENUE - 186 feet 6 inches

SOUTH CLAIBORNE AVENUE - 172 feet 0 inches

CANAL STREET - 170 feet 6 inches

NEW ORLEANS
1884
TEN NEWSPAPERS-
TEN UNIVERSITIES

In 1884, the year New Orleans held its first World's Fair, the fair handbook boasted that the city had ten newspapers and ten universities.

COLLEGES.

University of Louisiana, Common and Baronne streets.
University of Louisiana, Medical Department, Common between Baronne and Dryades streets.
University of Louisiana, Law Department, corner Common and and Dryades streets.
Louisiana College of Pharmacy, 300 Common street.
Jefferson Academy, 95 Conti street.
Jesuits' College, corner Common and Baronne streets.
Soule's College, St. Charles and Lafayette streets.
Southern University, 160 Prytania street.
Straight University, Canal, corner Tonti streets.
Valence Institute. 129 Valence street.

NEW ORLEANS NEWSPAPERS.

NAME.	PRICE, PER COPY.	POLITICS.	OFFICE.
Bee (French) . . . Daily	5 cents	Democratic	73 Chartres street
City Item . . . . "	5 "	Independent	39 Natchez street
Evening Chronicle "	5 "	Democratic	23 Bank Place
German Gazette . . "	5 "	Democratic	108 Camp street
Picayune . . . . . "	5 "	Democratic	66 Camp street
States . . . . . . "	5 "	Democratic	90 Camp street
Times-Democrat . "	5 "	Democratic	58 Camp street
Morning Star . . . ——	5 "	Catholic	116 Poydras street
Mascott . . . . . ——	5 "	Independent	68 Camp street
Figaro (Illustrated) ——	10 "	Independent	36 Natchez street

NEW ORLEANS NEWSPAPERS

Bee (French) daily - 5 cents - Democratic - 73 Chartres Street

City Item daily - 5 cents - Independent - 39 Natchez Street

Evening Chronicle daily - 5 cents - Democratic - 23 Bank

Place
German Gazette daily - 5 cents - Democratic - 108 Camp
Street
Picayune daily - 5 cents - Democratic - 66 Camp Street
States daily - 5 cents - Democratic - 90 Camp Street
Times-Democrat daily - 5 cents - Democratic - 58 Camp Street
Morning Star - 5 cents - Catholic - 116 Poydras Street
Mascott - 5 cents - Independent - 68 Camp Street
Figaro (Illustrated) - 5 cents - Independent - 36 Natchez Street

COLLEGES

University of Louisiana, Common and Baronne Streets.
University of Louisiana, Medical Department, Common
between Baronne and Dryades Streets.
University of Louisiana, Law Department, corner Common and Dryades Streets.
Louisiana College of Pharmacy, 300 Common Street.
Jefferson Academy, 95 Conti Street.
Jesuits' College, corner Common and Baronne Streets.
Soule's College, St. Charles and Lafayette Streets.
Southern University, 160 Prytania Street.
Straight University, Canal, corner Tonti Streets.

Valence Institute, 129 Valence Street.

The handbook highlighted the fact that New Orleans'
area of 155 square miles made it the largest city, landwise, in
the world. London, England, was second with 149 square
miles.

The city also boasted of having 650 miles of streets, and
was lighted by 4,599 gas lamps, 2,000 oil lamps and 482 electric lights.

WHEN THE LIGHTS WENT OUT ALL OVER NEW ORLEANS

On November 8th and 9th, 1882, New Orleanians who walked the streets at night (New Orleans' population at that time was 230,000) were literally left in the dark. The city owed the gas company $200,000 and refused to pay the bill. One might say the gas company was aghast, so they simply turned off the gas. This drastic action got both the immediate attention of the city fathers and quick payment of the bill.

MISSISSIPPI RIVER LIGHTS AND DEPTH

The mighty Mississippi River, from its beginning in Lake Itasca, Minnesota, to the Gulf of Mexico, travels 2,350 snake-like miles, making it the third-longest river in the world. The average depth northward from Baton Rouge is only 12 feet. From the river's entry into Louisiana to the Gulf of Mexico, the drop in elevation is approximately 100 feet. Because of this drastic drop, the river's speed increases considerably from this point on. The depth does likewise.

The deepest spot from beginning to end is recorded at 192 feet. This phenomenal depth for a river is located off the Algiers point in Orleans Parish.

Because of the swift current and sharp bends in the metropolitan New

Orleans area, there are three traffic lights to aid the flow of traffic. The lights located at the Governor Nicholls Street wharf and the one in Gretna are manned by licensed towboat pilots who are federal employees. The Westwego light is classified a repeater light and is controlled by the two manned stations. These traffic lights go into operation when the Carrollton Avenue gauge reaches eight feet on the rise and remain op-

erative until the level drops below nine feet on the fall (varies anywhere from two to six months in duration).

The only traffic lights on and the deepest spot in the Mississippi River are all located in metropolitan New Orleans. It is only apropos that the life and possible economic death of the community are in a sense controlled by this great river.

After many years of hard work, New Orleans is proud that its port has achieved its status as the No. 1 port in the U.S. and No. 2 in the world in exports.

CITY'S FIRST CHALLENGE

The first challenge encountered by the city of New Orleans after it was founded in 1718 was rather unique. When the first man died, the problem was how to properly dispose of him. When you live in an area that is below sea level, this was and still is a problem. The word cemetery is a Greek word meaning "to lie down". In 1718, in the French Quarter, when you dug a hole six feet deep, you instantly had 5 feet 11-3/4 inches of water. You could not lie down; you literally

had to float down. Can't you see, or better yet, hear your
loved one's last sounds being "gurgle, gurgle, gurgle"?

At first, to make the coffins sink faster, holes were drilled

in the bottoms. They did sink a little faster and partially eliminated the agony of the gurgling sound. Later, someone came
up with the idea of building a small house structure above

ground to overcome this traumatic experience. Because of
dampness, high humidity, and 60 inches of rain yearly, the
wooden structures did not last, so bricks were used. Finally,

to protect the bricks from the elements, they were plastered and then painted white as a symbol of purity.

These little structures sitting side by side look like houses, and hence the cemeteries of New Orleans became known as the "Cities of the Dead".

SULTANA

When the Civil War ended in 1865, the steamboat Sultana was sent to New Orleans to pick up Union soldiers who were in hospitals and Confederate prison camps. The ship was licensed to carry 376 passengers, including the crew. On the night of April 26, 1865, with a human cargo of 2,500 sick and weak men, the ship's boiler blew up. In a very short time, the entire ship was engulfed in flames. The horrible disaster took place during the night as the ship headed upriver

north of Arkansas. When the final count was made, 1,547 men had lost their lives. Until this day, the Sultana accident ranks as the most disastrous marine accident in history. Several dozen more lives were lost than in the highly publicized sinking of the Titanic.

ISLAND ON A PENINSULA

New Orleans is unique in many different ways. To name a few, the city is located on land that is almost totally below sea level. This is the reason interments in cemeteries in the Crescent City, for the most part, are done above ground.

The city receives approximately 60 inches of rain annually, necessitating collection of the water before it is pumped out. This is done by means of a man-made canal system. Because of this phenomenon, New Orleans has more miles of canals than Venice, Italy.

Several other unique or little-known facts are as follows: New Orleans is surrounded on three sides by water; therefore, the city, not normally thought of in this way, is located on a peninsula. When entering the city from the north, you must cross Lake Pontchartrain. From the east, it is necessary to cross the Rigolets and the Chef Menteur pass. From the south, one must cross the mighty Mississippi in order to enter the city. The only land connected to the City of New Orleans is from the west.

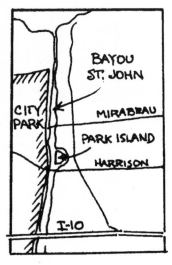

On the peninsula, there are many people who live on an island. This isolated area is called, "Park Island" subdivision. In order to reach their homes, those who live there, and others who visit or make deliveries are required to cross the one and only bridge leading to the island: this bridge is over Bayou St. John.

I guess you could say that it is rather unique to live on an island located on a peninsula that is almost totally below sea level.

FIRST RIVER FERRY
ONE HORSEPOWER!

In 1829, the first ferry boat to cross the Mississippi River at New Orleans was put into service. The unusual name given the craft was "the horseboat". When you think of it, it wasn't that unusual, for the catamaran type vessel's propulsion was

generated solely by a horse that walked in a circle, thereby turning the wheels which propelled the vessel.

Even though it worked as desired, it was short-lived, being replaced by the more efficient steam engine.

One could say, without contradiction, that New Orleans' first ferry boat operated on one horsepower.

LOUISIANA PURCHASE
NEW ORLEANS - COST $4,608

In 1803, Robert Livingston and James Monroe were commissioned by United States President Thomas Jefferson to purchase the City of New Orleans from France. They were authorized to spend no more than $10,000,000. After negotiations began, they were informed Napoleon was interested in selling not only the City of New Orleans but the entire Louisiana territory. Without authority, Livingston and Monroe negotiated to purchase the vast Louisiana territory for $15,000,000. On April 30, 1803, these two "horsetraders", without approval from the president, purchased 924,278 square miles of land, doubling the size of the United States

with the stroke of a pen. This negotiated real estate transaction was certainly the largest in terms of land area that had ever taken place in the world. Using the purchase price of 3-1/2 cents per acre, the City of New Orleans that Livingston and Monroe were authorized to spend $10,000,000 for cost a measly $4,608.

Upon learning of the transaction, Congress was appalled. They angrily said, "The people of this country will pay through their teeth for generations to come." The truth of the matter is, not one dollar of tax money was used to pay off the loan. The total cost of the Louisiana Purchase was paid by tariffs collected at the City of New Orleans.

U.S. CUSTOMHOUSE FACADE

The beautiful U.S. Customhouse located at 423 Canal Street took 33 years to build, due to the delay caused by the Civil War. The modified-Egyptian architectural, trapezoid-shaped building cost $4,179,854 and was the second largest federal building when it was finally completed in 1881.

Highlights of the magnificent structure are the four 36-foot 6-inch by 5-foot 8-inch by 5-foot 6-inch columns located over each of the four entrances of the building. Each fluted column was shaped from a mass of 105 tons, and each is cut from one piece of granite from a quarry in Quincy, Massachusetts. As a finishing touch, each column is topped by typically Egyptian capitals.

Theft of these embellishments is not a threat.

HISTORY RECORDED IN MANY WAYS

On April 25, 1862, a historical event was entered into a builder's journal with a bang. On that auspicious day, workers were high on a roof during construction of a plantation home. The location was an isolated section several miles upriver from the business district of New Orleans. As the men worked, they could see ships of Admiral Farragut's fleet silently moving into the harbor. As they banged fastening the flat roof planks  to the rustic roof beams, they heard another tremendous bang. Looking towards the river, they saw smoke from the recently fired cannons lazily floating around the ship as the projectiles raced to their targets. Knowing this to be of historical significance, the superintendent entered the event into the builder's construction journal.

Although the city fell to the federal fleet, the plantation house still stands. In 1862, the plantation house was sur-rounded by rows and rows of expensive crops. Today, the structure is located at 1328 Harmony Street, surrounded by rows and rows of expensive homes.

FAIRGROUNDS BETTING COMMISSIONER

Jesse James, a name familiar to all, was considered by those in his profession to be good at what he did, even if it was criminal.

His brother, Frank, was also known for the extraordinary results of his activities. So much so, the New Orleans Fairgrounds racetrack, after meeting with him,  without hesitation hired him as betting commissioner.

As a bandit, Jesse knew the odds against his remaining free forever were against him, but did his thing anyway. Frank simply knew everything about odds and used them to the track's advantage. In return, he was handsomely rewarded, plus he lived not only long, but a very comfortable life as well.

GENTILLY CLEANERS

An old gentleman advised that he and his wife go to the Gentilly Cleaners each and every Mardi Gras.

This is the term he affectionately used to describe the New Orleans Fairgrounds.

COLORFUL WEARING APPAREL

Those old enough to remember what some called the

good old days will recall the days when you could buy a Model T Ford any color you wanted, as long as it was black. There were no other colors to choose from. In the 1800's, the opposite was true in both ladies' and men's clothing. You could have any color you so chose, as long as you didn't choose black. Clothing colors in the 19th century were bright and gay. Someone jokingly said some were bright enough to hold a conversation.

A typical combination for a man's ensemble would have been bottle-green pants, tan coat and flowery multi-colored spangled-waist coat. Huge, fluffy ties were usually of yet another color.

One of the most popular bright colors in Louisiana was blue (indigo). The reason for the popularity was simple. Indigo was one of Louisiana's valuable crops.

It may seem hard to believe, but shoes, prior to the Civil War, were not available in right or left. When you purchased a pair of shoes, they were identical. There was one advantage; you could never put your shoes on the wrong foot when you had a little too much to drink. Of course, you could put your shoes and socks on, in that order, and everyone would then really know you were drunk.

"DIXIE"

The term "Dixie" we have all come to know as meaning the deep south was born in New Orleans prior to the Civil

War, or, as some Southerners call it, that unfortunate unpleasantness. Before the Civil War, the economy in the port city of New Orleans was literally bursting at the seams. The levee on the riverfront was lined for miles and miles with steamboats, and there was virtually no room left to store the cargoes brought to the port. Like the cargo, money was flowing like water, and the most prevalent bill was the $10 bill.

New Orleans, at this time in history, was still a divided city with Canal Street serving as the neutral ground between the Americans and the Creoles. After selling their cargoes and wishing to spend their money, the keel boatmen were inconvenienced since they had to use French money on the down-river side of Canal Street and American currency on the upriver side. The enterprising Citizens Bank, located on Toulouse Street, solved the problem. They simply printed the denomination ten (DIX is ten in French) on the face of each note both in English and French. The keel boatmen corrupted the word by saying, "We're going to New Orleans

to get those good old Dixies." Hence the deep south has been known as the land of Dixie ever since.

JAX ROOT BEER?

Yes, that's right, New Orleans did enjoy Jax root beer at one time. It came about because of Prohibition. Like other businesses in the city, Jackson Brewing Company looked for new ways of earning funds to make ends meet. Company management decided that those who did not or could not drink beer would be potential customers for Jax root beer.

As history points out, Jackson Brewing Company did survive. We can only surmise and would not be surprised to find out that Jax root beer was most helpful in making that difficult task possible.

COCKTAIL

New Orleans has long been famous as the home of civilized drinking. Facts are, there was a drinking establishment in New Orleans before there was a church.

New Orleans prides itself in being the birthplace of the ever popular cocktail which came about in the following way. There was a pharmacist named Antoine Peychaud, whose pharmacy was located on the corner of Royal and St. Louis Streets in the French Quarter. One evening after work, he and some of the members of his lodge held a meeting in the rear of his place of business. After the meeting, liquid refreshments were served by Peychaud. He experimented by using the double-ended measuring device he used to mix prescriptions. The piece of crockery used is called (in French) a

"Coquetier". The first cocktail was a brandy toddy with a dash of bitters and some secret Peychaud compounded to give it zest. The men were very pleased with this new taste, and from the instrument called the coquetier used to make the drink came the word "cocktail".

One of the city's most popular early cocktails was named for the much respected mayor, Louis Philippe de Roffignac who served from 1820-28. The Roffignac cocktail was made by pouring a jigger of cognac into a highball glass, adding a portion of raspberry or grenadine syrup, ice, soda and water.

It was said that anyone who could drink three of these potent cocktails could be mayor for the day.

WORLD'S LARGEST
DRAINAGE PUMPS

When you build a city that is:
(1) Built in an area mostly below sea level and,
(2) Receives an average annual rainfall of 58.16 inches, that city must definitely have a better-than-average drainage system.

New Orleans is just such a city, thanks to New Orleanian Albert Baldwin Wood. Because of this great mechanical engineer, New Orleans can rightfully boast of a superior drainage system, having the largest drainage pumps on the face of the earth.

Before the turn of the century, Mr. Wood designed, built and installed the first of the present twenty-two, 14-foot diameter pumps (the city currently has a total of 89 drainage pumps of various sizes). These pumps are large enough that, when they are opened for repairs, the open end is large enough to drive automobiles and trucks through.

CHURCH

Followers of Buddha celebrate their religious convictions in a temple. Muslims worship in a mosque, Jews in a temple or a synagogue. The Christians' house of worship is the church. From 1718 to 1803, New Orleans was, by law, 100% Catholic. Because of the city's early history, the majority of religious places of worship in the metropolitan area is now and always has been church. The very first church was located on the present site of the St. Louis Cathedral facing Jackson Square. The first structure was constructed of logs. It was half church, half warehouse.

Today, the city has two Christian cathedrals. The first is the St. Louis Cathedral which is also the second-oldest Catho-

lic cathedral in the country. The second is the Greek Orthodox Cathedral; it was the first Greek Orthodox cathedral in the country. That beautiful structure is located on Robert E. Lee Boulevard adjacent to historic Bayou St. John.

The tallest church steeple in the city is St. Stephen's, located on Napoleon Avenue and Camp Street, one block from Magazine Street. The overall height from  the ground to the top of the steeple cross is 210 feet.

New Orleans even has one church located in the middle of a cemetery. The original St. Mary's Assumption Church is located within Lafayette Cemetery No. 2 on Washington Avenue and Prytania Street. The small structure only seats 80 people. When the present, larger Irish Channel structure was built in 1858, the small wooden church was moved to its present quiet location.

WHAT PRESIDENT?

If you are ever asked the question "What president spent more time in New Orleans than all the other presidents combined?", you can turn the tables on the trick question by fielding the right answer. The correct answer is not a United  States President, but the Steamboat President.

POKER AND BOSTON

Poker and Boston are both card games, not a card game and a city, as one might suspect.

The Boston Club, having been founded in 1841, is New Orleans' oldest men's club. It derives its name, Boston, from the card game of the same name invented by a French army officer serving in Massachusetts during the American Revolution. The club's membership was made up of professional men who needed a private place to relax and unwind. What better way than by playing the ever-popular card game called Boston!

Poker, without question, is now, and has been for many years, the most popular card game in the country. Even though New Orleans was the first port of entry for Poker in the United States, it was not the first name given to the game of chance whose rules originated in Persia. The name Poker is a derivative of the French card game called Poque. (Chances are, some men finished the game feeling like a pig in a poke.) There were times when men left the card table, after relaxing and unwinding, minus their plantations and sometimes their entire fortunes.

THANKS, BUT NO THANKS!

Prior to the 1845 Louisiana Constitution, the office of governor was determined by the eligible citizens voting for the candidate of their choice. The names of the two candidates receiving the highest number of popular votes were laid before the legislature, and it chose the lucky winner.

In the 1920 gubernatorial election, Thomas R. Robertson received the largest number of popular votes, and Pierre Derbigny received the second-highest number. The legislature voted for Derbigny as their choice, even though Derbigny was second as the voting choice of the people. Upon learning of this, Derbigny declined the office saying, "If they (meaning the people) don't want me, I sure as hell don't want to serve them."

In 1828, Derbigny ran again and won both the vote of the people and the legislature. He served less than one year; he died on October 6, 1829, five days after he was seriously injured when his carriage overturned in Gretna, Louisiana.

Because of the embarrassing incident in 1820, the new constitution adopted in 1845 specified that the governor would be elected by the vote of the people.

CITY OF CANALS
VENICE OR NEW ORLEANS?

Without question, Venice, Italy, is known as the "City of Canals" by people all over the world. Venice, with its 28

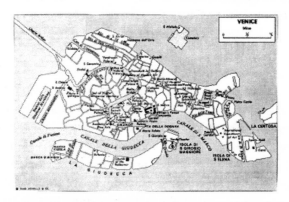

miles of canals, including its magnificent Grand Canal, is truly picturesque and historic.

Because the City of New Orleans is, for the most part, located on land below sea level, it has, by necessity, 87 miles of open canals, not counting its own "Grand Canal", better known as the Mississippi River. In addition, there are 85 miles of canals below the ground. These canals today are covered by what locals refer to as "neutral grounds".

New Orleans is also picturesque and historic, but it is not called the City of Canals, even though it has more than three times as many miles of open canals (not counting the mighty Mississippi) and three times as many miles of canals below ground level as Venice, Italy.

NEW ORLEANS'
FIRST STEAMBOAT
FIRST EXCURSION BOAT

The first steamboat to arrive at the Port of New Orleans arrived on January 10, 1812. The captain, pilot, engineer and six deckhands were greeted by thousands of curious onlookers who lined the river banks on both sides. Next came a royal reception by the city fathers and businessmen, who immediately saw the financial possibility of this new form of transportation. A slave, seeing a steamboat for the first time, was quoted as saying, "Old man river done met her master now."

The ship's owner, Nicholas Roosevelt, and her captain, Jay Baker, didn't lose any time in contriving ways to recoup their $38,000 investment in the steamboat named New Orleans. Shortly after arriving, they ran an advertisement in the paper, announcing excursions to English Turn and back. The fare was $3.00 per person. The ad pointed out that departure

would be at 10:00 in the morning, and the vessel would return at 3:00 in the afternoon. The advertisement also warned that "Passengers who desire to dine before that hour will kindly carry their own provisions."

The New Orleans was not only the first steamboat on the Mississippi River; it was also the first excursion boat.

SHOTGUN HOUSE

SHOTGUN HOUSE: A very narrow, long house with one door at the front and one at the rear.

The shotgun house came into existence when large num-

bers of poor Irish immigrants arrived in the city with nowhere to live. The riverfront was lined for miles with flatboats. Each had a long, narrow building to protect the cargo that was perishable. Because there was no mechanical power to take them back upriver, the barges were dismantled, and the structures on the barges were taken off and deposited on land near the

Irish section (Irish Channel). They were soon adopted as homes.

It was said that a shotgun could be fired through the front doorway and the shot

would go out the open back door without hitting anything;
hence, the name
shotgun house.

SHOTGUN
DOUBLE: The
same as above, ex-
cept two narrow,
long houses were
put together for
larger Irish families.

NEW ORLEANS
BIGGEST-TALLEST-DEEPEST-LOWEST
AND THE BEST

New Orleanians truly have much to brag about.

Can you name a city that has a domed structure equal to
the Superdome? There isn't one. The fact is, it is so big you
could fit the Houston Astrodome in-
side the Louisiana Superdome, with
plenty of room to spare. Now, that
is big!

When speaking of low, the
lowest point in the city is located at
the intersection of Lake Forest Boulevard and Bullard Avenue in New
Orleans East. It is eight feet below
sea level. Not one major city in the
U.S. can match that phenomenon.

On the other end of the spectrum, the Moriarty Monument, located in historic Metairie Cemetery,

is the tallest privately owned monument in the United States. It is also very beautiful, as well as historic.

From start to finish, the deepest spot in the mighty Mississippi River is located at New Orleans. Its depth between Algiers Point and the French Quarter is 191 feet deep.

The best we save for last. It is our humidity. You just can't get any better than 100%. 100% humidity in our city is not a rarity; it is a way of life.

1917 BATHING REGULATIONS FOR CITY BEACHES

At the last convention of the American Association of Park Superintendents, in New Orleans, the report of the Committee on Bathing Suit Regulations was read and the suggested regulations were adopted. The committee consisted of Harry S. Richards and Walter Wright, of Chicago, and Ralph Benedict, of Kansas City, Missouri. The rules adopted follow:

GENERAL

No all-white or flesh-colored suits permitted, or suits that expose the chest lower than a line drawn on a level with the armpits.

LADIES

Blouse and bloomer suits may be worn, with or without stockings, provided the blouse has quarter-arm sleeves or close-fitting arm holes, and provided bloomers are full and not shorter than four inches above the knee.

Jersey knit suits may be worn, with or without stockings, provided the suit has a skirt or skirt effect, with quarter-arm sleeves or closefitting arm holes and trunks not shorter than four inches above the knee, and the bottom of skirt must not be shorter than two inches above the bottom of trunks.

MEN

Men's suits must have skirt effect, or shirt worn outside of trunks, except when flannel knee pants with belt and fly front are used. Trunks must not be shorter than four inches above the knee, and the skirt or shirt must not be shorter than two inches above the bottom of trunks.

RESURRECTION FERN

Our area of the country is blessed with many beautiful oak trees. They are especially breathtaking in the early morning when the sun is just beginning to rise. The soft sunlight seems to enhance the beauty of the silvery moss that gracefully hangs from the branches.

There is another area of beauty that goes mostly unnoticed. If you look closely at the larger branches, you will see, especially after a rain, lush green fern that grows on the older trees. It is called "Resurrection Fern". The reason: it looks

dead during dry spells, but is "resurrected" soon after it rains.

JOHN CHASE

John was a multi-talented man who entered the newspaper world in 1925. He explained to his friends that, as a cartoonist, his drawings could speak for him. He acknowledged he certainly was not a speaker. Whenever John's editorial cartoons did have words, they were very few. Most of the time words were not used. He had the uncanny ability of conveying to his audience the happenings of the city through his forceful, even

though encapsulated drawings. John once told a friend movies were silent so why should his cartoons have sound?

In 1954, he became a trail blazer when approached by Channel 6 TV to try something new. He accepted the challenge and became the first United States television cartoon editorialist. He drew cartoon editorials on live TV for over a decade.

Chase could never spell, remembers his long-time friend and admirer Helen Dietrich. "He couldn't spell cat. He didn't care. He used to quote some cartoonist who said `damn the man who can spell a word only one way.'"

STREETS NAMED FOR
NINE DAUGHTERS OF ZEUS

Zeus, considered the highest of all Greek gods, was married to Mnemosyne, GODDESS OF MEMORY. As a dutiful mother she taught her nine daughters well. Each be-

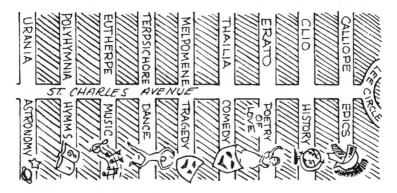

came a specialist in a different field.

In the early 1800's, during the period of Greek revival in the United States, the nine daughters (the Muses) were honored in the Crescent City by having streets named for them. Each of the nine streets crossed St. Charles Avenue (originally Nyades Avenue--God of Water) starting at Lee Circle (originally Tivoli Circle), going upriver. (See drawing.)

CHANGE
THE ONE SURE THING IN LIFE

Once you have been on this earth for a few years, you quickly learn that nothing lasts forever. Change, as they say, is imminent.

All one needs to do to confirm this truism is to look around the city of New Orleans.

At one time, New Orleans had:

Ten breweries, ten newspapers, over 100 cigar factories, several dozen streetcar lines, five railroad stations, as well as hundreds of seamstresses and outdoor watermelon stands. All neighborhoods had their own theatres and drug stores, and smokestacks could be seen everywhere belching black smoke. Then, it was called prosperity. That same smoke today is known as pollution.

Most of those listed above are few and far between. Some are holding on by their fingernails. Some no longer exist. But, a few things in New Orleans, including the Mississippi River, seem to keep on rolling along as they always have. The city has as many, and in some cases more, churches, universities, bars and cemeteries as it had 100 years ago.

SHAKSPEARE IRON WORKS
911 Girod Street

THE UNITED STATES MINT

It seems like we pray, learn, drink and then die. When we do, we are still in for change-from flesh and blood to plain old dust.

NEUTRAL GROUND

New Orleans is the only city in the U.S. that uses the term "neutral ground" for any street with a median. The way in which this term got started is as follows:

After the Louisiana Purchase in 1803, large numbers of Americans moved into the city. There was no love between the existing Creole population and the new arrivals. The Americans moving in located upriver from the French Quar-

ter. In the process, they left a wide expanse of land that served as exactly what the name implies -- neutral. The Americans and Creoles knew that if either crossed the neutral ground they would be subject to bodily harm.

As the city grew, miles of canals were dug to collect the approximately sixty inches of rain the city received each year. When they were covered over (canals remain below the ground), the term neutral ground was used to describe the area, just like the original neutral ground located on Canal Street in the downtown area.

WHAT IS A CREOLE?

Today, to discuss in a mixed group exactly what a Creole is is tantamount to opening a can of worms. If you look in Webster's Dictionary you will find many different possible definitions of the word.

The word "Creole" came from the Spanish word criollo, believed by the proud Spanish people to mean, "From the thigh of Jupiter". The word Creole was not used in the City of New Orleans until the Spanish took control of Louisiana in the middle 1700's. It did not take the French long to realize the word was a positive term. They adopted it and changed its spelling to the present "Creole".

How did the word Creole come to be misused? French Creole plantation owners sent their slaves into town to sell surplus crops, instructing them to advise the people that these were Creole products and, therefore, far superior to any others available. They were extremely successful in selling the fruits and vegetables raised by the Creoles. Thus, we came to have Creole tomatoes, Creole corn, Creole mules and Creole blacks. It was only logical that since they, the slaves, were also owned by the Creoles, they considered themselves to be Creole slaves.

A few years back, a very fine cook of Creole foods, named Leon Soniat, did a series of television shows on Creole cooking for a national network. Upon receiving the tapes, the network realized he was a white man and refused the series under the title of "Creole Cooking" because it was felt that, nationally speaking, people think of Creoles as being black people. It is easy to understand why others would like to be considered Creoles. "From the thigh of Jupiter", creme de la creme, piece de resistance, who would not like to be counted in that number?

TOWBOATS

The term "towboat" is a misnomer on the Mississippi River. As you will note from the drawing, barges on the Mississippi River (only river in the world where this is done) are pushed instead of towed, as implied in the

word "towboat".

One Mississippi River towboat has the power to push a sufficient number of barges having the capacity of a quarter million bushels of grain, or enough 12" pipe to lay 40 miles of pipeline. It would take 100 diesel locomotives with 100 freight cars each to carry the same amount of material.

There are 118 barge lines operating out of the Port of New Orleans, accounting for nearly half (48%) of the port's total water-born commerce in an average year. On any given day, 50% of all of the barges in the United States are in the area of the Port of New Orleans.

A WALK ON WATER

In this instance, we are not writing about a passage in the Bible. What we are referring to is what happened on the Mississippi River in 1899. The year was a record breaker in low temperatures throughout the nation. It had been bitterly cold. Ice formations that started in Minnesota made it all the way to the Gulf of Mexico. The ice referred to in newspaper articles was massive enough that reports were made of men who literally make their way across the river by moving from one large ice chunk to another, finally reaching the other side.

The title "A Walk on Water" is maybe a stretch of the truth, but a true statement nevertheless, considering the water they walked on was frozen.

Those who were not brave or dumb enough, depending on your outlook, crossed the river by way of the ferry boats to get a close-up look at the parade of ice. Knowing the passion of New Orleanians for parades, they did a brisk business.

It appears that local entrepreneurs never let a disaster deter them in their ultimate goal of earning some gold. It was also reported that a number of steamboats discontinued carrying freight when Old Man River broke through the levees and turned a prosperous plantation owner into an instant pauper.

Yes, that is one thing that will never change. One man's misfortune has always been another man's good fortune.

WHAT A REVOLTING DEVELOPMENT THIS IS!

Have you ever wondered where the old saying "What a revolting development this is!" came from? Although there is no surefire way to prove how it came about, the following bit of historical fact is as good an indication of its birth as any.

On March 9, 1949, the New Orleans Brewing Company, Inc., located at 418 Jackson Avenue, went out of business. The company dumped 93,000 gallons of beer down the drain after deciding that disposal of the beer stocks was cheaper than the cost of prolonged storage and refrigeration.

For the next week, New Orleans undoubtedly held the world title of having more inebriated rats than any other city in the world.

**37TH BIRTHDAY
GREATER NEW ORLEANS BRIDGE**

Although a bridge to cross the mighty Mississippi River at downtown New Orleans was proposed as early as 1824, it was not until April 15, 1958, that the dream of connecting the east and west banks finally became a reality. The man most responsible for completion of the bridge was Captain Neville Levy. For many years, Captain Levy, with monumental human opposition, almost single-handedly spearheaded the project. After many years of constant battling, it was only natural that he anxiously awaited the official dedication. Nothing could or would stop him now. Channel 6 TV, still in its infancy, was equally anxious to cover the dedication ceremonies live from the center of the span. The TV field reporter covering the event was Alec Gifford. The big moment had finally arrived, and Captain Levy started the dedication ceremonies. Instantly, almost if on cue, a thick heavy fog covered the entire bridge, including Captain Levy, TV news reporter Alec Gifford, and the many dignitaries who had assembled on the span. Although Captain Levy could not be seen on TV he could at least be heard, so the program went on. This unfortunately did not last long. The fog horn located on the superstructure in the center of the span began to bellow. Not only could Captain Levy not be seen; now he could not even be heard. In spite of the human opposition and the opposition of the weather, the bridge was dedicated as planned.

From almost the beginning of its existence, the Greater New Orleans Bridge (now named the Crescent City Connection) has had the distinction of being the most heavily traveled bridge in the United States. Prior to the opening of the second span, it was affectionately called "the most patriotic bridge in the United States, the car strangled spanner".

NINE O'CLOCK CURFEW

Until shortly after the Louisiana Purchase, New Orleans was a fortified city. The wall surrounding the French Quarter was anchored by five small forts.

Each night, at exactly 9:00 p.m., the curfew cannon, located in Place d'Armes, shattered the silence of the evening. The thunderous explosion served as a reminder to all slaves that they were required by law to be in their quarters. It also signaled the gatekeepers to lock the main gates located on Pontchartrain Road, the approximate location of today's U.S. Mint on Esplanade Avenue near the river. Once locked, no one was allowed to enter or leave without special authority until daylight the following morning.

A visiting writer wrote, reference the city and the surrounding wall, "Now that I have been in the city long enough, I know why they built the wall. It is to keep the good people out, for the city is occupied by sinners of almost every known vice."

LADY SALES CLERKS

D. H. Holmes went into the retail business in 1842. In doing so, his became the very first department store in the United States. Mr. Holmes was a very progressive merchant. In 1845 he also instituted the very first department store home delivery. He was far advanced in many areas reference the retail business.

During the Civil War, 60,000 men from Louisiana joined the Confederacy in defense of their newly adopted country. This mass exodus left a void for retail stores in the area of sales people. The agressive and progressive retailer filled the void by hiring the first female sales clerks. He found them to

be highly efficient, as well as extremely reliable.

The D. H. Holmes ladies department was also the first in the United States to have ready-made ladies dresses hanging on the racks by size for immediate sale. Prior to that time, all ladies dresses were made to order only, after a fitting was completed.

OPERA WAS "FINANCIAL" MUSIC TO HIS EARS

Yet another innovation instituted by Holmes was to keep his department store open nights during the opera season. He advertised that he offered this as an extra service to his customers. He was also smart enough to know who had the largest amount of money to spend.

UNIQUE SMUGGLING TECHNIQUE

Some ladies used their great pillory skirts in a way unforeseen by the enemy. Having lots of room to hide things, they used these skirts to smuggle medicine and military supplies through federal lines.

BREAKING TRADITION

In 1899, Proteus, God of the Sea, was forced to cancel

its parade because of inclement weather. You would think that the god of the watery sea would not allow water to cancel his parade, but it did. Realizing they were going to have to reschedule their parade, they had an emergency meeting and decided to parade the Friday after Mardi Gras (during Lent).

The parade did roll, but, to the krewe's amazement, the streets were virtually empty. Like the old lady in the hamburger commercial who said, "Where's the beef?",  Proteus members said, "Where's the crowd?"

Yes, New Orleanians, as previously stated, are truly tradition-minded people.

HALF AND HALF??

Half and half is good if you are drinking coffee at Cafe' du Monde. Half and half is not good when your property is half in Orleans Parish and the other half in Jefferson Parish. This may seem like an impossibility, but it exists until this day.

Most believe the 17th Street Canal divides Orleans and Jefferson Parishes. But the canal is not really the true dividing line. Houses and business places on the New Orleans side of the canal are actually partially located in both parishes. At several of the West End restaurants, slot machines at one time could be found in the restaurants, but only on the Jefferson Parish side. Slot ma-

chines being illegal in Orleans Parish, only the space on the Jefferson side was used for slots.

17TH STREET CANAL?

Why, do you ask, is there a 17th Street Canal, but no 17th Street the entire length of the canal? The answer: At one time there was a 17th Street in the Carrollton area. The street name was changed, but the title of the canal, until this day, remains the 17th Street Canal.

WE'RE NUMBER ONE

On March 8, 1967, when the New Orleans Saints ticket office opened its windows at 8:00 a.m. Al Whiteman, upon purchasing his tickets, became the very first New Orleans Saints season ticket holder. Al proudly states that he has been a loyal Saints supporter since the very beginning, and is equally proud to hold the title, "No. 1 Saints Season Ticket Holder". Al was followed by Calvin Long of Poydras, Loui-

siana. Hundreds of eager fans waited in line throughout the cold night wrapped in blankets. The weather might have been cold and damp, but Al and Calvin would allow nothing to dampen their spirits as they anxiously awaited the entrance of the New Orleans Saints into the NFL.

SILENT ENEMY

Prior to the invention of Captain Henry Miller Shreve's snag boat, steamboats that carried passengers and cargoes on the Mississippi River and its tributaries were as vulnerable to being sunk as American ships were during World War II. The silent culprits in World War II were the highly efficient German U-boats and their deadly, unseen torpedoes.

Steamboats were sunk by an equally silent adversary that had no compassion for its victims. The steamboat nemeses were huge submerged logs just below the water line. Like the German torpedoes, the snags, even if seen at the last moment, didn't allow time to avert disaster.

From 1822 to 1832, the loss of steamboats and their cargoes caused by snags amounted to $1,743,500, plus an untold number of lives of both men and beasts.

Through the invention of Captain Miller's snag boat, the once deadly nemesis was completely eliminated.

The Steamboat New Orleans, built by Robert Fulton, was not only the first on the Mississippi River; it was also the first to be sunk when it struck a snag. The accident happened in 1813, just below Baton Rouge.

NEVER ON A FRIDAY

Prior to the Louisiana Purchase, Creoles adhered to the practice of never being married or buried on a Friday. The reason: Friday was the official day public hangings were held in Place d'Armes (today's Jackson Square). The hangings took on a festive atmosphere and were always well attended. All citizens, young and old, were encouraged to attend by the city's leaders. They felt it was a means of discouraging future crimes. Rather than trying to compete with the hangings, the Creoles simply avoided Fridays for weddings and burials.

EMPTY PEDESTALS?

It is truly ironic that even though New Orleans, a city blessed with an overabundance of statues, there is not one statue commemorating the largest and most famous Mardi Gras in the United  States to be found anywhere in the city.

It is equally flabbergasting that, with the port being the number one rung in the city's economic ladder from the very beginning until today, there are no statues to commemorate the marine industry.

That is, unless you look upon the armless, headless man painted white along the riverfront close to the ticket office  behind Jackson Brewery. It supposedly represents the river, but for the life of me, I have never been able to associate the statue with any facet of the river.

ORLEANS PARISH

Of the 64 parishes in the State of Louisiana, Orleans is one of the very smallest in size, yet the largest in population. The following are the 1990 Census population statistics.

Five largest parishes by population:
1. Orleans 496,938
2. Jefferson 448,306
3. East Baton Rouge 380,105
4. Caddo 248,253
5. Calcasieu 168,134

WELL, I'LL BE

Because New Orleans encompasses all of Orleans Parish (it is the only city in Louisiana that covers the entire parish), it may be surprising, but true, New Orleans is less than five miles from the Mississippi state line (as the crow flies).

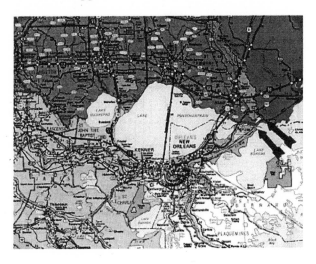

CHAPTER FOUR

CITY OF CELEBRATION

INTRODUCTION

The Crescent City is truly a city of celebrations. Every known form of celebration is enjoyed to the fullest. Because of the city's multiethnic and religious makeup, parades, festivals, fairs and celebration of feast days of the saints alone make for what seems like a never-ending party. The Irish have been celebrating St. Patrick's Day in a big way since 1809. The Italians pay tribute in numerous ways to St. Joseph and St. Rosalie. The Vietnamese, the city's newest arrivals, wasted no time in joining the pack. Each year, they stage a colorful, well-attended, ethnic celebration for their proud people. In recent years, the African-American contingency have joined in the fun. For many years, African-Americans were known basically for being the Mardi Gras Indians and celebration of voodoo. In years gone by, the Indians used to perform only on Mardi Gras and St. Joseph's Day. Today, they still take part in those two events, but now perform at the Jazz & Heritage Festival, as well as entertain at conventions throughout the year. There are plans in the making for a year-round Mardi Gras Indian museum. African-Americans today stage celebrations throughout the year. There is also a full month each year set aside when they and the rest of the citizens take part in learning of and celebrating their heritage.

Local citizens, as well as visitors from around the world, take part and enjoy the two largest celebrations of their kind in the world. Mardi Gras is billed as the "largest free show on earth", while the Jazz & Heritage Festival is far larger than the next three jazz festivals combined anywhere in the world.

Besides all of the different ethnic celebrations each year,

the Children's Museum conducts a children's world's fair. Many believe it to be the number one children's function during the year. Each year, 15 different countries are highlighted. When children arrive at the fair, they are issued a passport. As they go to each of the countries to learn of its customs, music, dance, food and costumes, they are required to show their passports and have them stamped, just as travelers do when going to foreign countries.

Not even death can escape a celebration in the city of celebration. We must give the Irish immigrants credit for that unique form of celebrating. Irish wakes, lasting three full days, included food, drink and story telling. The latest jokes were also shared at these solemn gatherings. The Irish were also the originators of celebrating death with musical funeral parades. True, it may have taken thousands of years after his death, but even King Tut, the Egyptian boy king, could not escape our love of celebration. Citizens, believing he never received a proper send-off, staged one for him in the form of a jazz funeral. It was held on January 15, 1978, to commemorate the closing of the Treasures of Tutankhamun exhibit in city park.

On December 9, 1852, citizens felt that three great American statesmen, John Calhoun, Henry Clay and Daniel Webster, never received a proper send-off. It didn't matter that none of the three were Orleanians. A lenghty funeral parade was held in their honor. Representatives from every state of the union took part. As a reminder of that colorful historical event, part of the funeral car, specially designed and built for the occasion, was displayed in the Louisiana museum for many years.

Yes, if we will go to those extremes in celebrating death, you know what efforts we are willing to put into celebrating life.

CITY OF CELEBRATION

Natives, as they say, are so close to the trees they don't seem to see the forest. On the other hand, those who visit or move here from elsewhere sometimes realize the Crescent City is truly a city of celebration. The two main factors for this phenomenon are as follows.

1. Years before the Civil War, New Orleans had 68 different nationalities living within the metropolitan area. The French and Spanish, before the Louisiana Purchase, introduced and perpetuated the all-popular carnival and Mardi Gras celebration traditions. Both also were heavily involved in music, dance, galas and dinner parties where both music and dance were enjoyed to the fullest. Without question, the city is also the parade  capital of the world. With just carnival and Mardi Gras, an estimated 1,500 parades have been staged.

Each of the 68 nationalities wishing to perpetuate its country's identity, introduced its own ethnic type of celebration, including parades, spring fiestas, galas, etc. A few examples of these would be the St. Patrick's Day festivities, which included a parade, St. Joseph's altar and parade, and St. Rosalie celebration, which included a procession. African-Americans participated with the Zulu parade and Mardi Gras Indians. In more recent years, the Vietnamese have joined the merriment with their own celebration using traditional costumes, colorful, moving dragons emitting smoke from the nostrils, and, of course, a parade. In fact, the old saying in New Orleans is "When in doubt, why not stage a parade?"

As already pointed out in Chapter One, General Andrew Jackson did just that.

2. In addition to the multitude of nationalities, New Orleans people are, for the most part hard working. It is an accepted fact that people who work hard play equally as hard.

Yes, as they say, Laissez les bon temps rouler. When we get off from work, we will be there.

PARADE CITY U.S.A.

New Orleanians' addiction for parading is unequalled, not only in the United States, but anywhere in the world. Parades have been recorded in the Crescent City as early as July of 1734 when the Good Sisters of the Ursuline Order dedicated their first convent.

N.O. first parade 1734

True, the largest number of parades is during the Carnival season and Mardi Gras, but parades for every occasion are spread throughout the year. There are parades for the Sugar Bowl, St. Patrick's Day and St. Joseph's Day, for the Spring Fiesta and at Christmas time to name just a few. Throughout the year, jazz funerals take to the streets carrying to their final resting places those who have contributed to this world-renowned music that was born in New Orleans in the early 20th century.

With tongue in cheek, the following story is in reference to New Orleanians and their love of parades. When New Orleans was a very young city, a man was convicted of a heinous crime. He was sentenced to be hung by his legs in Place d'Armes (now Jackson Square), where the local citizens could pass and scoff at him. The sentence was carried out as ordered, with two guards posted beside him at all times. After many, many hours of hanging in this most uncomfortable position, plus a continuous flow of angry people passing, one of the guards heard the man mumbling faintly. He leaned over and heard the man singing very softly, "I love a

parade". It seems that New Orleanians' love of parades has never diminished and apparently never will.

FIRST MARDI GRAS PARADE IN U.S.
NEW ORLEANS, LOUISIANA OR MOBILE,
ALABAMA???

Early New Year's morning, 1830, in Mobile, Alabama, a group of young men were heading home after a fun evening which included plenty of libation. They passed a general store where merchandise was displayed out front. The group picked up shovels, rakes, hoes and cowbells, and walked down the street to the home of the mayor, where they raised holy hell. The mayor invited them in, sobered them up, and offered the

ringleader, Michael Krafft, a suggestion, "Next year, why not organize yourselves and let everyone have fun?" Michael formed a group called the Cowbellion de Rakin Society, after the instruments they used to raise hell. On New Year's Eve the next year, with costumed riders on floats lit by flambeaux, a New Year's Eve parade was held, to the delight of the crowds. Success was such that it was repeated as an annual event each New Year's Eve.

In 1856, some members of the Cowbellions, now living and working in New Orleans as cotton brokers, decided to hold a Mardi Gras parade to entertain the crowds in New Orleans, as they did in Mobile on New Year's Eve. They chose the name of the Greek god, Comus, the God of Revelry. They spelled it with a "C" to give it an English look. Since they would be a crew of men, they spelled it krewe as a semblance of Greek influence. On February 24, Mardi Gras 1857, starting at 9 p.m., the first Mardi Gras parade with floats, costumed riders and

Feb. 24, 1857
First Comus Mardi Gras Parade

flambeaux, all borrowed from Mobile, was held in the United States to the total enjoyment of the crowds.

Ten years later, 1867, the Cowbellion de Rakin Society in Mobile moved their New Year's Eve parade to Mardi Gras day.

MARDI GRAS INDIANS

As colorful as the African-American Mardi Gras Indians are, their origin is equally clouded and obscure. Many years ago, a historian interviewed many of the chiefs to see if he could track down their origin. He started by interviewing Brother Tilleman, Chief of the "Creole Wild West" tribe who was regarded as the "King of the Chiefs". Tilleman felt quite sure the tribes had their beginnings in the late 1800's. When speaking with chiefs of other tribes, they all disagreed. They believed the tradition dates back to the mid 1800's, but had no way of backing up their beliefs.

Although there is no concrete evidence that they are right, you may wish to share their sentiments as I do, based on the following: When people of various ethnic groups leave their homeland, they almost invariably bring with them whatever they can, especially their ethnic celebrations. This serves to remind them and at the same time express pride in their proud ethnic background. An early example of this is Mardi Gras. The French founded Louisiana, and almost from the beginning they celebrated Mardi Gras in their new surroundings. With the Irish came their beloved St. Patrick's Day celebration. The Italians brought with them celebrations of two of their beloved saints, Joseph and Rosalie. The proud Germans were no different; they had their Oktoberfest.

Looking back in history, we find the first slaves to arrive in Louisiana were brought from the Guinea coast of Africa. Shortly after, shipload after shipload were sent from the French colonies of West Indies and the Caribbean Islands. History also documents there were black men from Trinidad as early as 1847, who, on festive occasions dressed and performed as Indians. They daubed themselves with red ochre and were known as the "Red Indians". In Trinidad, various neighborhoods developed symbolic rivalries and created appropriate music and dance steps. The most important song of the New Orleans Mardi Gras Indians is ironically called, "My Indian Red". The similarities of the Trinidad Indians and New Orleans Mardi Gras Indians in costume, music, dance, esoteric language, etc., are too numerous to be considered a coincidence. Therefore, it is very possible, and highly probable, that some of those African-American men who celebrated by being Indians in Trinidad in the mid-1800's one way or another found their way to New Orleans. Like every other ethnic group, they wished to retain a tie with their homeland. They were able to do this through their Indian costumes. At the same time, they added something new and picturesque to the New Orleans Mardi Gras celebration.

NEW ORLEANS INDIAN TRIBES OF THE PAST AND PRESENT

UPTOWN
Wild Magnolias
Black Eagles
Cheyenne Hunters
Golden Arrows

Iroquois Hunters

DOWNTOWN
The White Eagles
The Yellow Pocahantas
Golden Stars
Cherokee Hunters

Yellow Jackets

"INDIAN BATTLEFIELD"

At one time in Mardi Gras history, many Indian tribe members carried real weapons. In their hands, they carried razor-sharp spears and equally sharp hatchets. Added protection, concealed in their costumes, were knives and loaded guns. Mardi Gras for the Indians became the day to settle all grudges. All during the year when there was trouble between two men, you would hear them say, "Wait till Mardi Gras, I'll make you bow." This meant that when tribes passed each other during Mardi Gras and did not bow to the other, thereby acknowledging the superiority of the rival tribe, they would end up on the Indian battlefield located on South Basin Street and the New Basin Canal - now site of Greyhound bus and Railroad terminal at Howard and Loyola Avenues.

During the course of the day on Mardi Gras, chiefs and braves increased their bravery 100 fold by fortifying themselves with large quantities of firewater. Because of this practice, there were very few bows, leading to bloody confrontations late in the evening on the Indian battlefield of honor. Many combatants were seriously injured. Some never left the field alive. City police did not intervene at the Indian battlefield on Mardi Gras. Conditions deteriorated to the point that Mardi Gras Indians were not allowed to participate in Mardi Gras. After some years had passed and tempers cooled, the tribes came back, and today physical combat on the Indian field of honor is only a memory. Today's competition is strictly of a creative nature. Today's tribes participate for self-satisfaction and enjoyment by displaying their exquisite, individually designed costumes. They revel in entertaining the huge crowds they draw and mesmerize with their rhythmic music, exotic dancing and eye-catching colorful costumes. Today's Mardi Gras Indian tribes, like the original tribes of old, are out to have a good time and are no longer hostile to each other. They have turned full circle and today can be seen entertaining not only on Mardi Gras and St. Joseph's Day but also at the Jazz & Heritage Festival, numerous conventions in New Orleans, and who knows where else in the future.

BLACK IDENTITY IMPORTANT

An Uptown tribe broke tradition by allowing a white college student of Norwegian nationality to mask with the group for two years. When the Saint Joseph's Day parade was inaugurated in the Spring of 1972, tribes all over the city, with one exception, participated. The tribe with the white student was banned by the other tribes from participating. The conclusion drawn from this incident is that black identity plays an important role in these organizations.

RENEGADE INDIANS

Some black men dress in Indian costumes and parade alone. They are called renegades by the Mardi Gras Indian tribes.

CARNIVAL'S FIRST QUEEN
1870! ALMOST!

Comus, New Orleans' first Mardi Gras krewe, was so successful with its parade and ball, that a group of enthusiastic, Carnival-struck Orleanians decided it was time to increase the enjoyment of the celebration by forming a second Carnival krewe. The name chosen was Twelfth Night Revelers, representing twelve days after Christmas (also known as Little Christmas), January 6th, the official starting day of the Carnival season.

Just as Comus added new wrinkles to the Mardi Gras festivities, the new krewe had a few innovations of its own to add. On the evening of January 6, 1870, the Twelfth Night Revelers opened the Carnival season with a nine-float parade that was equal in splendor and pageantry to the previous Comus parades. Following the nine floats, many maskers followed on foot, dressed in the colorful costumes of Europe, Asia, Africa and America.

After the parade, a ball was held at the world-famous French Opera House on Bourbon Street. The leader of the Twelfth Night Revelers, who was called the Lord of Misrule, reigned over the ball. After the two tableaux were completed, the Lord of Misrule led the court members in a grand march, followed by four court fools carrying an immense king cake. The grand march, the first of the new wrinkles planned by the new krewe (and copied by almost all krewes that followed), met with tremendous success. Everyone in the packed opera house waited with great anticipation to see what other surprise the Lord of Misrule had up his royal sleeve.

Up until this time in Carnival and Mardi Gras history, there had never been a queen of the celebration. In fact, prior to this time, all parades, balls and tableaux were planned and staged by men. Women did not participate in any fashion until after the tableaux, when ladies were summoned from the audience to take part in the dancing.

And now the great surprise of the evening was about to be unveiled. The first queen in the history of the New Orleans Carnival was about to be chosen, crowned, and put upon a pedestal to be admired. The huge king cake was brought out for all to witness the proceedings. When the cake was prepared, a golden bean had been placed inside. The court fools were to slice generous servings of the cake and pass them to the ladies who waited patiently. The lady receiving the piece of cake with the bean inside would become queen.

However, all did not go as planned; the court fools lived up to their roles. No doubt because of their overindulgence

12th Night Revellers Ball,
where first Queen of Carnival was to be chosen — But wasn't !

in liquid refreshments to prepare them for the merriment of the evening, they did not politely pass the slices according to plan, but, instead, dropped them in the laps of the stunned recipients. In fact, some cake was even thrown at the ladies by the more-intoxicated jesters.

The ladies of the court were, to say the least, appalled at the proceedings and rightfully so. In protest, the lady who did receive the slice containing the bean swallowed it, and the evening ended without a queen being crowned.

It was not until the following year, 1871, when the court fools were better behaved, that a queen, Mrs. Emma Butler, was crowned when she found the golden bean in her slice of cake.

Selection of a queen at the Twelfth Night Revelers Ball through the use of the king cake is still practiced today. In place of a real cake, a huge artificial cake with little drawers is used. One drawer holds a golden bean and each of the others a silver bean. The lady selecting the drawer with the golden bean is crowned queen, and those choosing drawers containing silver beans are the maids.

**REX
PAYS SILENT RESPECT**

Through the course of Mardi Gras history, there have been many unusual and unique happenings that have taken place. On February 16, 1904, one such incident occurred. As Rex, the King of Mardi Gras, rolled down the parade route on St. Charles Avenue, all 12 bands in the parade gave a silent tribute to Arthur Landry. Arthur was the stepson of world-renowned Dr. Rudolph Matas. Matas is known all over the world as the Father of Vascular Surgery. He was also Dean of Surgery at Tulane University. Landry's untimely death occurred several days prior to Mardi Gras. As a form of respect

to those who were in mourning at Dr. Matas' home, all bands marched in silence for several blocks before and after passing Dr. Matas' home at 2255 St. Charles Avenue.

This is the only time in recorded Mardi Gras history that this courtesy was extended to anyone by any carnival organization.

FLAMBEAUX
NEW ORLEANS MARDI GRAS TRADITION

According to Webster's Dictionary, a flambeau is described as a "flaming torch". The better term in New Orleans would be "EXCITEMENT".

The first nighttime parade in New Orleans with a theme, parade route, floats, masked riders plus flambeaux was the Krewe of Comus, February 24, 1857. The first Comus parade had only two floats, Comus, the God of Revelry, on one, and Beelzebub in the mouth of a volcano on the second. The floats were followed by hundreds and hundreds of masked revelers, most of them dressed as devils. The city at that time had no electricity and very, very few whale-oil lamps to illuminate the streets. To light the way for New Orleans' first nighttime parade, several hundred flambeaux were lit at 9:00 p.m. at the corner of Julia and Magazine Streets. When ignited, the sky lit up as though the entire city was on fire. It drew the people of New Orleans to it like moths to an open flame. Although the city did not catch on fire, the nighttime parade lit by flambeaux did ignite enthusiastic feelings about nighttime parades that are as popular today as the first nighttime parade in 1857.

KREWE OF COMUS FEB 24,1857

This year marks the 138th year that Mardi Gras flambeaux have been in use. Yes, Comus, the God of Revelry, who introduced them to the New Orleans Mardi Gras, will once again illuminate his nighttime parade with the ever-popular and excitement-building flambeaux.

NEW ORLEANIANS ARE "TRADITIONALISTS"

From the time of the first Rex Parade in 1872, the four major Mardi Gras Krewes, Rex, Comus, Proteus and Momus, have used what has been considered the traditional Carnival and Mardi Gras parade route. The route is as follows:

Down St. Charles Avenue and around Lee Circle past Gallier Hall (the old City Hall) to Canal Street and on to their ball locations.

It was also customary from the very first Rex parade for the king of Mardi Gras to propose a toast to city officials at City Hall.

When the late deLesseps "Chep" Morrison, undoubtedly New Orleans' most popular mayor (1946-1961), completed his new and futuristic Civic Center, he was as proud as a peacock. The tall, modern City Hall was its brightest jewel. Chep no doubt thought that by re-routing the Carnival and Mardi Gras parades right through the Civic Center (fully a mile out of the way), the traditional toast could be made in front of the new City Hall, and this would allow him to show off his latest accomplishment. The captains of the various krewes were not especially keen on this idea. In fact, they were downright opposed to it. Chep was a strong-willed person and reminded the captains that in order to obtain a parade permit the city's full cooperation was required. Chep held the trump card. The captains of the various krewes had no other choice. They did, although reluctantly, change their routes and passed in front of the new City Hall. In a sense, the mayor simply blackmailed the captains into carrying out his wishes. When parade time rolled around, the masses of people who attended the parades were not as receptive or intimidated into accepting the new route. Like stubborn mules, they would not accept this departure from tradition. Although the krewes changed their parade route to please the mayor, the people did not show up at the new Civic Center. The old die-hard traditionalists simply went to Gallier Hall, the old City Hall (which was still on the parade route), where they had gone for so many years.

As the old saying goes, if you don't succeed the first time, try and try again. The next year, the city again tried to entice the multitudes to come to the new Civic Center. The results of the second attempt were less successful than the first. Because of the wishes of the people, through non-participation, the city allowed the captains to go back to the old traditional parade route. One old timer said, "Chep would have had an easier time passing a new tax (and you know how New Orleanians hate taxes) than he had trying to change one of our sacred Mardi Gras traditions."

You could say the people of New Orleans sang "Don't Mess with My Parade Route" long before the popular song "Don't Mess with My Tu Tu" was written.

EUROPEAN CARNIVAL VS. LOUISIANA MARDI GRAS

Carnival was born in Europe about 5,000 years ago. After all this time, the celebration in Europe is still alive and well. Carnival is still celebrated in Greece, Spain, France, Germany, Italy, Switzerland and Holland, to name just a few of the countries.

Even though carnival in North America was introduced by France and later by Spain, and even though the purpose of the celebration is the same in Europe and North America, there are a number of differences in the way we celebrate. Some of the differences are as follows:

BEGINNING OF CARNIVAL

In Europe, the official starting date for carnival is St. Martin's Day, November 11th, at precisely 11:11 AM. This tradition was started by German dukes, the real kind, in Cleve, Germany, in 1382. The reason for the date and time is that the number 11 is considered the fools' number. Therefore, the celebration of fools should start on the 11th day of the 11th month at precisely 11:11 AM.

In our area, the official starting date of carnival is January 6th. It is also called twelfth night, or little Christmas. This is the day the three wise men brought gifts to the Christ child. In parts of Europe, January 6th is still the date on which children receive their "Christmas" gifts.

WHERE CELEBRATED -- EUROPE VS. LOUISIANA

In Europe, you will find the carnival celebration in the heavily populated Catholic areas, many being located on rivers and other waterways.

This is exactly the same in Louisiana. Carnival and Mardi Gras have been, and are still, celebrated in predominantly Catholic areas of the state, with many of them located on waterways.

CARNIVAL ORGANIZATIONS

In Europe, each carnival group is headed by a council of eleven. (There pops up that fools' number again.) The top man on the council is equal to the captain of our Mardi Gras krewes. He has absolute power and is responsible for selecting the Carnival Prince. The selection of the prince is highly secretive. No one knows who the prince will be until the appropriate time. The youngest member of the council of eleven is called the baby. His face is placed on the body of a naked baby and publicized in the media. The oldest carnival organization in Europe is Momus. The oldest carnival organization in Louisiana is Comus. In Europe, the prince has to be a native-born man in each community. One oddity in the European royalty for carnival is the fact that the "princess" of carnival has always been a man. Almost always, that is. For a short time when Hitler was in power, this practice was discontinued. Hitler would not tolerate any of his supermen serving as princesses of a fools' celebration. Once Hitler was out of the way, the practice of a princess being a man was reinstituted.

It is interesting to note that in the New Orleans Mardi Gras the Zulu queen for a number of years was also a man. He was a female impersonator who used the stage name of "Queen Corinne".

In the larger European cities where there is train service, the prince of carnival always arrives by train to start the carnival season. Over the years, the king of Mardi Gras arrived in various ways the Monday before Mardi Gras. Originally he arrived on a royal yacht by way of the Mississippi River; in later years by train. When airplanes became popular, he arrived in that manner. Today, the king of Mardi Gras arrives on the Monday before Mardi Gras (called Lundi Gras) by way of the Mississippi River as he did originally.

PARADES

In Europe, all parades are held in the daytime, and are held on only two days, the Sunday and Monday before Ash Wednesday. Tuesday, the big day we call Mardi Gras (translated Fat Tuesday) is of less importance in Europe. Only minor celebrations of varying types are held in different communities.

In Europe, floats are much smaller in size. Costumed riders are on floats only if they are of functional value. There is one exception to this, and that is in Cologne, Germany. They do use large floats, carrying men in costume, who throw the most expensive boxes of chocolate candy, fruit and flowers. These men are influential leaders of business and industry in the community.

There is no one float builder in Europe who makes all of the floats. Each float is made by individual groups from the carnival club, vo-tech schools, or simply neighborhood people. Each group, of course, tries to outdo the other by building unique, automated floats.

Each parade has a theme selected by the council of eleven. Unlike the Louisiana carnival and Mardi Gras -- they do not use the term Mardi Gras -- the European carnival is planned entirely for the local people. In Holland, for example, a very small country, there is a standard language. There are also 50 different dialects. People living 50 miles apart do not understand the dialect of their closest neighboring town. Throughout Europe, visitors are not considered important, because they would not understand the theme, which usually pokes fun at the local political leaders and other local events.

Smaller communities, unable to finance parade floats, find other means to express themselves. For example, one city has an all-bicycle parade. Many imaginative designs of bikes of every conceivable size and shape make up the entire parade.

In Venlo, Holland, there is one traditional float used every year. It is a float depicting Hell, with a huge boiling pot and Lucifer in his flaming-red costume. Members of the political and military arena who did not fulfill their promises, or did things they should not have done, are thrown into the pot, in effigy, to the delight of the crowd. If the misdeed was of a lesser nature, the effigy of the party in question is simply set on the edge of the red-hot pot.

Financing of the parade is spread out in the following way: the carnival club pays part of the expense, the municipal governments furnish some of the financing, neighborhoods who build floats pay for the materials, and also do the construction. The other means is by passing a hat in the crowd at the beginning of the parade.

THROWS

There is no throwing from floats in most of Europe as already explained. The throwing is done by the crowds who attend the parade and shower the floats with confetti and serpentines.

In the early Louisiana Mardi Gras celebration, confetti, bonbons, and flour were thrown by the crowds at and to each other, long before there were parades where throwing from floats became an integral part of the celebration.

DOUBLOONS

This is a local contribution to the carnival and Mardi Gras celebration. In Europe, they do not use doubloons, but do have a carnival coin that is made of aluminum. It is not thrown; it is used to purchase beer during the carnival celebration. The coins are sold by the carnival clubs. This is another way they earn money to offset the cost of the parade. In Louisiana, carnival clubs also sell doubloons to members, and the profits are likewise used to offset the cost of the parade.

COSTUMES

In Europe, almost everyone wears a costume. Yet, there are no masks allowed other than painted faces. Many costumes are worn as a means of poking fun at political and military leaders, church dignitaries, religious orders or whoever is the object of their ridicule.

BALLS

Carnival balls in Europe are unlike present-day New Orleans Mardi Gras balls. They are basically costume dances with a paid admission, same as the balls held in New Orleans before the first Comus ball in 1857.

MISCELLANEOUS

Throughout Europe, many store owners decorate the fronts of their buildings for carnival. Butcher shops display plucked chickens and ducks in their windows, each wearing a different carnival costume.

The carnival season throughout Europe is called the fifth season. It begins on November 11th and officially ends with the burning, hanging, drowning, burying in effigy, or some other destruction of the prince of carnival.

There is no king cake tradition in Europe as there is in Louisiana. But, Ash Wednesday is celebrated the same in both places. On Ash Wednesday, a priest makes a cross of ashes on a Christian worshiper's forehead while saying, "Remember, man, from dust thou came and to dust thou shall return."

Another tradition in Europe is the eating of herring prepared in vinegar on Ash Wednesday. This is to remind people of the 40 bitter days of fasting in preparation for the glorious and holy celebration of Easter.

UNORTHODOX
BASEL, SWITZERLAND

Originally, Basel was a highly populated Catholic city. The Bishop of Basel had a break with Rome because of conflicting beliefs. There is a carnival parade in Basel today as there has been for hundreds of years. But it is now held the Monday after Ash Wednesday, during the Lenten period. On the evening of the parade, the city's electrical department turns off all non-essential electrical service, leaving the entire city in the dark. At precisely 4:00 AM, a parade lighted by men carrying flambeaux winds its way through the darkened streets to the total enjoyment of the costumed crowd. The sides of the floats are lighted from the inside with torches. There are scenes poking fun at local political, military, and church leaders. No doubt, the Catholic church gets its share of ridicule in this manner.

NEW ORLEANS' FIRST
ALL SAINTS DAY CELEBRATION

St. Peter Street Cemetery, established in 1721, was the city's first burial site. It was purposely built at St. Peter and North Rampart Streets because (at that time) that was the out-skirts of the city. The population steadily grew, and, by the 1740's, the cemetery was completely surrounded by resi-dences. The citizens went to the city fathers and told them of their displeasure of sitting in front of their homes and look-ing into the unappealing cemetery. In order to kill two birds with one stone, the city fathers convinced the wealthy citi-zens to donate bricks for a fence that would also serve as a back wall for above-ground burial vaults. They then talked the poor into building the structure.

The job was completed and dedicated on November 1, 1743 (All Saints Day). For the occasion (just as we do today

more than 250 years later), citizens used the old European All Saints Day tradition of honoring the deceased by visiting their last resting place, cleaning and decorating the tombs with fresh flowers, saying a silent prayer and savoring fond memories.

NEW ORLEANS
IRISH WAKES -- MUSICAL FUNERALS -- SECOND-LINING

Many years before there was music called "jazz", Irish funerals were accompanied by musical groups. This tradition was brought to the Crescent City by the Irish immigrants, who represented 20 percent of the city's population in the first half of the 19th century.

IRISH WAKE

The hard-working Irish immigrants had great love of life and equal love of a suitable send-off for their loved ones when the time came. After death, the body was properly prepared and displayed in the home of the deceased's family for three days. The body was placed in the living room on what was called a cooling board. The two-foot by eight-foot cooling board was draped with beautiful Irish linen that touched the floor on both sides. During the warm months (which is the majority of the time in New Orleans), to offset the eventual offensive odor, items with great fragrance such as gardenias, roses, sweet olive branches, orange blossoms, etc., were placed under the cooling board, behind the linen drape. This being the great occasion that it was, neighbors loaned the bereaved family their finest chairs, curtains, tablecloths, lamps, etc., so the home would be suitably furnished.

Friends and neighbors were notified of the wake through the church bulletin, by word of mouth, posters displayed on corner posts and frequented spots such as markets, coffee houses, etc. There was an endless supply of food available for all such occasions. Great quantities of alcohol were also consumed, some in the form of toasts made in honor of the

deceased. During the wake, the Irish women in attendance, unable to control their emotions, from time to time would take part in what was known as Irish wailing. This was a high-pitched, penetrating  sound that once heard was never forgotten. As the funeral time got closer, the louder, more frequent, and higher the pitch the wailing became.

MUSICAL FUNERAL

The final day having arrived, all was made ready for the funeral. First, the procession went to the church for solemn services and finally to the cemetery for burial. On the

way to the cemetery, the funeral hearse, adorned in black and pulled by four black horses, was followed by the family and a group of musicians, who were in turn followed by friends and acquaintances. On the way to the cemetery, the music was slow and solemn. Once the body was entombed and the final blessings were given, the band played joyful, fast and loud music. This was to acknowledge that the deceased had achieved the ultimate goal of meeting his maker.

It is said that no Irish gentleman in his right mind went directly home from the cemetery. Proper protocol was to stop at a local pub to "wash away" the cemetery dust.

Irish musical funerals preceded jazz funerals by scores of years. It was not until the first quarter of the 20th century that there was even music called jazz.

SECOND-LINING

Second-liners are simply those who follow behind the family and musical group in the funeral procession (or parade). Because New Orleans is semitropical, with almost daily afternoon  showers in the summer months, many carried umbrellas to protect themselves from the rain or to shade themselves from the sun. Because of the heat and intense humidity, men and women kept their handkerchiefs in their hands to mop their brows constantly.

Like jazz, it is not known exactly when second-lining began or who was the first person to decorate his or her umbrella or to wave his or her handkerchief while second-lining. It is not only conceivable, but highly probable, that decorated umbrellas, waving of handkerchiefs and second-line dancing got their starts by the same fun-loving, hard-working Irish people who gave the city the first recorded musically accompanied funerals.

Please keep in mind that it is a known fact that the Irish drink when they have liquor available and dance when they hear music. Each of these ingredients was available at both the Irish wakes and funerals.

NEW ORLEANS IRISH
AND
THE FIRST ST. PATRICK'S DAY
CELEBRATION

New Orleans, from its very beginning, has been blessed with Irishmen amongst its citizenry. Over the years, they have been involved in virtually every aspect of the community. In the beginning, it was an Irish engineer who assisted Bienville in laying out the streets for the newly founded city. Today, New Orleans is blessed in having a dedicated, highly capable Irishman named William J. McCrossen, now retired, who served our city diligently for 13 years as fire chief. Sandwiched between can be found a list of fiery members of the cloth, numerous outspoken newspaper publishers, progressive and zealous mayors, doctors, lawyers, and merchants, as well as a multitude of pub operators. To assure law and order, the city's first chief of police was fearless David C. Hennessey, who gave his life in the line of duty.

The first recorded celebration of these God-fearing, hardworking, hard drinking, and loving people, honoring their beloved St. Patrick, took place on St. Patrick's Day in 1809, three years before Louisiana received statehood.

Although it was the first recorded celebration, it was a colossal event. Among those in attendance were the governor of the state and almost every important member of the legislature. The mayor of the city was there, along with important judges and politicians from miles around. The list of private citizens who attended undoubtedly was used for many years as a list of who's who in New Orleans.

During the course of the evening, virtually everyone attending the festive function made a toast. They toasted St. Patrick, Ireland, beautiful colleens, plus leprechauns and the shamrock. They toasted America, George Washington, the State of Louisiana, and on and on and on, until an American named Thomas Robertson proposed a toast that pleased the Irish present to no end. In fact, his toast was the highlight of the evening, and was printed in the newspaper the following day. Robertson's toast was as follows:

"To the people of Ireland, may they be as successful in establishing their own independence as they were conspicuous in aiding the accomplishments of the independence of the United States."

In reading of the pandemonium that went through that great hall after this toast, one can only envision the fiery red smiling faces and the feeling of pride of those attending the city's first St. Patrick Day celebration.

Everyone was so pleased with the affair that a St. Patrick's Day Club was organized, with Mr. John Duncan being elected its first president.

In 1996, New Orleans will celebrate its 187th St. Patrick's Day celebration. Let us lift our glasses of green beer (or anything else that is green) in toast that we might have many, many more.

STRANGE BUT TRUE

The St. Patrick's Day celebration in the Irish Channel is centered around the Parasol Bar.

It is rather unique, since in the middle of the Irish Channel a German family owns and operates the Parasol Bar.

IRISH PRIDE
MALE AND FEMALE

The first statue dedicated to a female in the United States was dedicated to Margaret Haughery of New Orleans. She died in 1882. Her statue was dedicated in 1884.

The first world champion of sports from North America was New Orleans' own Paul Morphy (family name was originally Murphy). He was crowned chess champion of the world in 1858.

For many years, the New Orleans Fire Department has been manned by dedicated Irish Firefighters. On Washington Avenue between Camp and Magazine Streets, the edge of the Irish Channel was the location for Engine Number 23. The building now houses the New Orleans Fire Department's museum. Who better to direct a fire department museum than Fire Chief McCrossen? For 13 years this distinguished, proud Irishman protected the citizens of the city.

CHRISTMAS
NEW ORLEANS' FIRST CHRISTMAS
CELEBRATION
FEUX DE JOIE AND MIDNIGHT MASS

CHRISTMAS EVE TRADITION "Feux de Joie" ("Fires of Joy")

Although we do not know the exact date New Orleans was founded, there are historical records of the first Christmas celebration. It occurred on Christmas Eve, 1718, the same year that New Orleans was founded. Fifty settlers began the celebration on the banks of the mighty Mississippi River, adjacent to Place d'Armes, with the original Feux de Joie (fires of joy) that had its beginning in Europe long before Louisiana was discovered. The popular Feux de Joie was started as a symbol of inter-village friendship, and the flames lit the way to the traditional midnight mass. At the appropriate time, the people filed into the first temporary Church of St. Louis. The structure occupied the same site as the present St. Louis Cathedral. The rustic chapel was illuminated, as well as warmed, by a fire in a potbelly stove that was chock-full of pine knots. The priest, in his finest mass vestments, celebrated the first recorded "masse de minuit" - midnight mass - in the city of New Orleans. Assisting at mass were Governor Jean Baptiste Lemoyne Sieur de Bienville (founder of New Orleans), joined by the French and Canadian settlers of the city. Also in attendance were a few sailors, a score of soldiers and some shabbily dressed weary traders and trappers.

PLANTATION TRADITIONS

Many plantation masters owned homes in the French Quarter. On Christmas, small children of slaves were allowed to hang their stockings on the mantel in the master's house the week prior to Christmas. On Christmas morning, the children went to the house and collected their stockings that were

filled with peppermint, candy hearts and a blue-back spelling book.

Christmas was a big day for the children and was followed by another tradition they enjoyed equally as well. On New Year's Day, the children would stay close to their homes and wait until the master blew his trumpet. With the first rat-a-tat-tat, they would run full speed to the front of the big plantation house and line up single file. From the front porch, the master would give each child a picayune (coin), which they saved to purchase some bananas from the fruit man when he made his regular trip to the plantation.

CHRISTMAS
MARDI GRAS TRADITION OF OLD

Although not related to the birth of Christ, December 25th was looked forward to by a small select group of young New Orleans socialites.

Awakening bright and early Christmas morning without the need of an alarm clock was not a difficult task. It was on this day the young ladies of the social register anxiously awaited a visit from royalty in the form of a duke of a Mardi Gras krewe, whose job it was to deliver a box containing a dozen red, long-stem American Beauty roses to each of the excited ladies.

When the duke arrived and presented the box of flowers, the young maiden's heart rate increased substantially, and her hands trembled. With great anticipation, she unwrapped the box and searched through the roses for the much-cherished parchment scroll that announced whether she would be a maid of the krewe's upcoming Mardi Gras ball or if she would be summoned to serve as queen of its Mardi Gras festivities.

Upon receiving the good news on Christmas morning, with the Christmas decorations of red and green surrounding her, the young maiden had visions not of sugar plums dancing in her head, but a crown signifying she had been selected to be queen.

CHRISTMAS AND NEW YEAR'S TRADITIONS OF THE PAST

Christmas to the Creoles was a religious festival and a family day that began with the entire family attending midnight mass. Several hours before midnight, to help pass the time while waiting to leave, the head of the house prepared and served the traditional Christmas Eve drink of eggnog. This was drunk to ward away the chill of the night as the family walked to church.

Papa Noel did visit on Christmas, but he only filled the children's stockings with small inexpensive gifts.

Christmas day was one of gastronomic delight as witnessed by a typical Christmas menu.

BREAKFAST

Sliced oranges, hominy and milk, broiled tenderloin

steak, potatoes a la Creole, omelette a la Creole, rice cakes, Louisiana syrup and cafe' au lait would be served.

DINNER

Gumbo file', radishes, cheese, pickled onions, courtbouillon, mashed potatoes, beignets d'oranges, roast turkey, oyster stuffing, cranberry sauce, baked yams sliced and buttered, stuffed tomatoes, lettuce salad with French dressing, old-fashioned chicken pie, plum pudding, mince or apple pie, pineapple sherbet, homemade sponge cake, jelly and pound cake, apples, oranges, bananas, grapes and an assortment of nuts and raisins, homemade Creole bonbons, cheese, crackers, raspberry, marmalade and cafe' noir would be the menu.

SUPPER

Cold turkey with cranberry sauce, cheese, jelly, small cakes and tea would be on the table.

TOYS ON NEW YEAR'S DAY

New Year's day for the children was more exciting. Just as the infant Jesus received gifts from the three kings in early

January, so, too, did the Creole children receive their gifts on New Year's day. Children rose very early in the morning and, with great pride, delivered to their parents a large pale pink envelope. In the envelope was a sheet of pink paper trimmed with tinsel and pictures of fat cherubs ringing silver bells. Each child painstakingly wrote a verse stating he would be good and wished mama and papa a happy and prosperous New Year. In return, they were showered with many, many gifts.

Immediately after breakfast, they dressed in their new clothes and went to visit their grandparents. For this special occasion they were allowed in the first parlor, which was normally off limits to children. Here they received more gifts; then they were on their way  to visit godparents, uncles, and aunts. By the end of the day, all relatives had been visited, and the children's small arms ached under the weight of the gifts they received at each stop.

CREOLE INGENUITY

Creoles considered Christmas the most important holiday of the year with Christmas dinner being the most important "eating event" of the year. Countless weeks (not hours or days) were spent in preparation of the food that was to be served at this auspicious occasion. Because there was no refrigeration to aid them in keeping the flowers fresh and because they had no control over the weather that determined when the flowers would bloom, Creoles were compelled to devise a means that would guarantee blooming roses on the dining room table on Christmas. This dilemma was solved by the following ingenious procedure: The last rosebuds

grown in the fall were cut, then the stems were dipped in paraffin, and the entire flower was wrapped in tissue, and then stored in a cool place. Early on Christmas morning, the rose stem was recut, and then the rose was placed in hot water, which allowed them to bloom for that one important day.

When the Creole family sat down to the gala Christmas dinner, they not only had their favorite foods and wines, but were assured of having roses, their favorite flower, on the table.

Creole ingenuity was equaled only by their love of food and the beautiful surroundings on the most important event of the year.

CHRISTMAS TRADITIONS

With Christmas being celebrated throughout the world, it is only apropos that the various Christmas traditions we enjoy began in various geographical areas of the world.

CARDS

The Christmas card tradition got its start in England in 1842 when artist William Egley designed a card and had 100 of them sent to his friends.

The Christmas card tradition was introduced in the United States by a German immigrant (printer) Louis Prange in 1875. More than 2 billion Christmas cards are sent annually in the United States.

MANGER

St. Francis of Assisi is said to have started the custom in Greccio, Italy, on Christmas Eve 1223 when he arranged the stable with real persons and animals as actors. Since that time, the crib has been a familiar site in both churches and homes throughout the Christian world.

CANDLES

Christmas candles may have had their origin in the Jewish Feast of the rededication of the temple (Hannukah). In the middle ages, it was customary to set up a candle in the center of a

1984 WORLD'S FAIR

laurel wreath and keep it burning on Christmas Eve and every night during the season.

The custom was particularly cherished in Ireland, where candles were placed in the windows of homes on Christmas

Eve during the period of religious supression so that any priest in the neighborhood might be guided to the house and possibly celebrate mass there. The custom was brought to America by Irish immigrants in the 19th century. From it derives the present-day custom of decorating homes and public buildings with lights of all kinds.

CAROLS

The earliest known hymn in honor of the nativity is "Jesus Light of All the Nations" written by Saint Hilary of Poitiers in 368 AD. Until the 13th century, all hymns in honor of the nativity were generally solemn and strictly religious. The true Christmas carol, lighter, informal and jovial, was born in Italy, Example: "Adeste Fideles" (O Come All Ye Faithful) was written in 1274 by a Franciscan monk named Saint Bonaventure.

DECORATIONS

HOLLY: According to legend, Christ's crown of thorns was made of holly leaves, and thus the custom of fashioning the Christmas wreaths began.

MISTLETOE: Was believed to have many miraculous powers. Among the Romans, it was a symbol of peace, and it was said when enemies met under it they discarded their arms

and declared a truce. From this comes the popular custom of kissing under the mistletoe.

POINSETTIA: The most popular of all Christmas plants was discovered in Mexico in 1828 by United States Ambassador, Dr. Joel Roberts Poinsett.

CHRISTMAS TREE: The custom of decorating Christmas trees was borrowed from the Ancient Romans, Egyptians, and Druids who thousands of years before Christianity adorned trees with gilded apples, cakes and lighted candles to worship their gods.

The forest people of Germany are credited with being the first Christians to decorate Christmas trees. The custom became very popular and spread to other parts of the Christian world. Princess Henrietta decorated Vienna's first in 1816.

The United States first Christmas trees were decorated by German immigrants in the 1840's. By 1856, the tradition had caught on, so much so that President Franklin Pierce had one set up in the White House that year. In 1895, President Grover Cleveland installed the first electrically lit indoor Christmas tree. In 1923, President Calvin Coolidge installed the first lighted tree outdoors at the White House. Prior to electric Christmas tree lights on strings, candles were used. They were placed in holders and clipped on Christmas tree branches. It was customary that whenever candles were lit on a Christmas tree, one member, usually an older member of the household, was assigned the job of staying close to the tree with a bucket of water to prevent a disastrous fire.

New Orleans' entry into the tradition of decorating Christmas trees began in the mid 1850's. Because of New Orleans' geographical location, the traditional fir tree was not available. No problem - New Orleanians simply substituted locally available trees such as cedar, sassafras, Japanese plum, althea and the indigenous wax myrtle.

Christmas trees were such a novelty in the Crescent City in the 1850's that the ladies of St. Paul's Episcopal Church actually charged admission to view their tree.

Although the Christmas tree tradition was not started in the United States, the U.S. does receive credit as being the first country in the world to set up lighted Christmas trees in public places.

CHRISTMAS CAROL
"SILENT NIGHT"

In the early morning on December 24, 1818, Father Josef Mohr, pastor of a small Catholic Parish in Oberndorf, Austria, received devastating news. The little church's organ had broken and there wasn't sufficient time to fix it for Christmas Eve's popular midnight mass. Father Josef kept his cool; he knew of his congregation's love of music and especially the accompaniment of the little organ. He knelt in silence in the empty church. What could he do to fill the void caused by the broken organ? His thoughts reverted to early in the morning when he blessed a newborn baby. This no doubt triggered an idea that would eliminate his dilemma plus, unbeknown to him, in time bring joy to hundreds of millions of people throughout the world.

In what might be considered quicker than a wink, he wrote three stanzas of the Christmas carol entitled "Silent Night". Without a doubt, the first of the three stanzas was inspired by his earlier act of blessing the newborn child. Once the lyrics were written, he rushed over to the home of his good friend and church organist, Franz Gruver. Within several hours, the lyrics and music were united.

Later that same evening, with the church packed for midnight mass, Father Josef and Franz accompanied themselves with guitars and played and sang "Silent Night" for the first time.

If there is a moral to the story, it would be, with a positive attitude and belief in the Almighty, every stumbling block can be turned over and made into a stepping stone.

COLORS OF CHRISTMAS

Just as the colors of the American flag -- red, white and blue -- and the Mardi Gras colors of purple, green and gold have meaning, so do the colors of Christmas.

They are:

GREEN: The continuation of life through the winter and the Christians' belief in eternal life through Christ.

RED: Signifies the blood that Jesus shed at his crucifixion.

CHRISTMAS
CANDY CANE

An ingenious, creative candy maker, wishing to make a candy that would be symbolic of Christmas, came up with the idea of the ever-popular "Christmas candy cane".

The candy is extremely hard and white in color. The white is symbolic of the virgin birth and the sinless nature of Jesus. The hard texture represents the solid rock foundation on which the church was built.

The shape of the candy was purposely made in the form of a "J", representing the precious name of Jesus. It also serves as a reminder of the staff of the "Good Shepherd".

The pure white "J" was, by design, stained with one large and three small red stripes. The larger stripe represents the blood shed by Christ on the cross so those Christians who follow His teachings should have, as promised, eternal life. The three small stripes represent the Holy Trinity, the Father, Son and Holy Spirit.

Unfortunately, over a period of time, the Christmas candy became known simply as a candy cane. But, the meaning is still there for those Christians who follow the teachings of Christ.

CHRISTMAS CELEBRATIONS THROUGHOUT LOUISIANA

Without question, Louisiana is a beautiful state. We have greater diversity than possibly any other state. Aside from

deserts and snow-covered mountains, virtually everything else can be found in Louisiana. Couple this fact with mild weather year 'round, and you will find natives and visitors looking at the Pelican State as heaven on earth.

The saying in Louisiana is now and always has been, "laissez les bon temps rouler." That is, let the good times roll. And roll it does all year long with festivals, fairs, carnival & Mardi Gras parades, plus every other form of entertainment conceived by man.

If I were a visitor and had to pick one season over all others to come to Louisiana, it would be during the Christmas season. The friendly, cheerful, fun-loving people of Louisiana at this time of year become even more friendly and cheerful. Every area of the state has unique ways to celebrate the holy season of Christmas. For a verbal tour of some of the highlights throughout the state, read on, you all.

Our first stop will be in the state's oldest city, Natchitoches. And you thought New Orleans was the oldest! Founded in 1714 on the Red River, Natchitoches was originally expected to grow and become one of Louisiana's largest cities. Unfortunately, the old Red River changed its course and left Natchitoches high and dry. But let this not discourage you from visiting Natchitoches. The reason-the small community with its magnificent fireworks, put on by the world famous Zambelli Fireworks Company, is as grand a fireworks spectacle as this writer has ever witnessed. Following the fireworks is a Christmas lighting display, where one million lights look like two million because of their reflecting in the Cane River. This is a sight once your eyes have seen will never leave your memory.

Just north of Natchitoches, located on the Red River, is Shreveport. It is here the American Rose Center is located on 118 acres. Roses from all 50 states are on display year 'round and highlighted at Christams. At this fesitve time, 500,000 lights shine in numerous sculptured religious figures, plus the Statue of Liberty, Eiffel Tower, and many, many others. Of course, there is a live manger scene, and Christmas music fills the air as your eyes soak in the beautiful surroundings of this 118-acre Garden of Eden.

Alexandria, located in the center of the state, has a Christmas celebration appropriately called "Christmas at the Cross Roads". Being hilly in this part of the state, as you drive at night you cannot take your eyes off the breathtaking view. It seems everyone in Alexandria not only decorates their homes with lights, but outlines their driveways and sidewalks with lights as well.

In Lake Charles, in the southwest corner of the state, you will see the unusual in the form of a 120' Christmas tree on a barge in the middle of the lake. The season opens with Santa's arrival by water, followed by fireworks, and then the lighting of this unique tree. Because this is Cajun country, you would not want to miss the stage production of "The Cajun Night Before Christmas".

East of Lake Charles, we find the oil hub of Louisiana, Lafayette. In this rich community, there are many events. Unfortunately, our space allows us the highlights of only two. The first is a 37' high "living Christmas tree". That's right, a "living Christmas tree". It is made up of 350 singers, with a specially designed lighting and sound system. At the base of the tree, 40 accomplished musicians accompany the singers. Once your memory bank records this scene, it too, will never be erased. The second event is equally spectacular and impressive. It consists of a breathtaking ride on a steamboat down the Vermilion River towards the Gulf of Mexico. The river is lined on both sides with magnificent homes. This area is appropriately called "Millionaires Row". These good folk graciously decorate the rear of their houses for the benefit of the river traffic.

Speaking of water tours, steamboat rides on the Mississippi River between New Orleans and Baton Rouge on Christmas Eve allow viewing of a European Christmas tradition in Louisiana dating back to 1718. A month before Christmas, families in St. John and St. James Parishes build huge wooden structures. The celebration is called "Feux de Joie" - Fires of Joy. Hundreds of structures, from the conventional tepee style to elaborate replicas of plantation homes, steam engines and railroad cars, etc., are built on the levees. On Christmas Eve, all of the structures are ignited to the delight of the huge crowds that flock to the area to witness this old and beloved Christmas tradition. The purpose of the fires was twofold. One, to light the way to midnight mass. Two, to wish those they would not get to see on Christmas a very holy season's greeting.

Our last stop is New Orleans, the culinary capital of the world. Here, people do not eat to live, but live to eat. Every restaurant is at its peak at this time of year. Local artists show their skills in spectacular displays of ice carvings. The carvers use everything from hand chisels to chainsaws. The French Quarter is a beehive of activities. Numerous musical entertainers are on the narrow and cheerfully decorated streets every day during the Christmas season. The Sunday night before Christmas, you can participate in caroling in Jackson Square. Each person is given a candle and a song sheet as he enters the square. A feeling of friendship during this event is sure to give you goose bumps. If you wish to visit homes and patios in the French Quarter, this is by far the most colorful time of year to do so. Some of the famous historical homes in New Orleans, decorated and open to visitors at this time of the year, are the Beauregard House, the Herman Grima House, and Long Vue House and Gardens, to mention just a few. If you have the time, please do not pass up a visit to Jackson Barracks, for it has the largest collection of antebellum homes anywhere in the United States. All are appropriately decorated for this most festive of seasons. New Orleans , like almost every town of any size in Louisiana, treats its citizens and visitors to a magnificent Christmas parade. During the entire month of December, City Park (the nation's third largest) has its annual "Christmas in the Oaks" extravaganza. In 1988, 300,000 people took in the breathtaking sights and absorbed the beautiful heart-warming Christmas sounds. Visitors have a choice of a casual walk or leisurely drive through the 1.7 miles of eye-catching decorations. The park rightfully boasts of having the largest collection of giant moss-laden oak trees in the U. S. The trees are lighted with both flood lights and a multitude of small Christmas lights. The trees are also decorated with hundreds and hundreds of sparkling ornaments that are up to 12 feet long. They have to be huge in order to be in proportion to the giant trees. The botanical garden has 50 large Christmas trees, each decorated by a garden club or school. Keen competition between both groups has fostered trees from the contemporary to the unique in the form of a "Who Dat" Christmas tree, appropriately decorated in black and gold in honor of the New Orleans Saints football team. This year, another new innovation will be introduced. Visitors will be able to take a ride at night on the park's miniature train through a maze of lighted trees and ornaments.

The finale of Christmas in the Oaks is held the weekend after Christmas. Radiofone's snowland consists of 40 tons of manufactured snow that is pumped into a slightly hilly area for the enjoyment of children from six months to 66 years young. People are urged to bring their pets, as past experience shows they enjoy it as much as the humans.

Yes, the above is only the tip of the holiday season celebrations in Louisiana. It is a time of good cheer. To repeat as we say in Louisiana, "laissez les bon temps rouler", especially during this joyous and holy holiday season.

ORIGIN OF WEDDING TRADITIONS

There are numerous bridal customs practiced, but rarely understood, by those who are getting married. For the most part, wedding traditions often stem from ancient times.

THE WEDDING RING

The ring's circular shape has been a symbol of unending love since the days of early Egypt.

THE RING FINGER

This custom has two origins, an ancient belief that a vein in the third finger, left hand, ran directly to the heart, and a medieval religious practice of placing the ring on three fingers to symbolize the Father, Son, and the Holy Spirit of the Trinity.

THE WHITE GOWN

White did not become a symbol of bridal purity until the beginning of the 20th century. In Victorian times, white was a sign of affluence; in early Roman times, it was a symbol of celebration.

THE BROKEN GLASS IN JEWISH CEREMONIES

At the end of a Jewish wedding, a wine glass is wrapped in a cloth and placed on the ground, and the groom smashes the glass with his foot, not for good luck as commonly believed, but as a reminder of the destruction of the holy temple and of other travails which the Jewish people should not forget even in the midst of a joyous celebration.

CARRYING THE BRIDE OVER THE THRESHOLD

To demonstrate her reluctance to leave her family, a Roman bride had to be dragged into her new home by her groom. Ancients also believe that evil spirits linger at the door of the new house, so the groom lifted the bride over the threshold to protect her.

FIREWORKS

Orleanians' passion for fireworks is equaled only by their love of parades, po boys and the ever-popular New Orleans Saints. The one big difference: celebrating with fireworks has been a tradition in and around the Crescent City much, much longer than any of the passions listed.

Just as New Orleans is out-of-step with the rest of the country in many areas, the economy being one, New Orleans for many years used fireworks at Christmas and New Year's Eve long before they were used to celebrate the Fourth of July.

The first recorded use of fireworks in New Orleans was early in the 19th century. On December 20, 1803, the American flag flew over Louisiana for the first time. On that auspicious day, 27 years after independence was achieved, locals became Americans. Being the

fun-loving people they were, they celebrated with military parades, fire drills by the militia, and thunderous salutes by the artillery, not to mention numerous parties, balls and general jollification evoked by the day's excitement. The evening ended with-what else?-a loud, colorful, mesmerizing fireworks display.

December 23rd took its place after 1814, for it was then that Andrew Jackson, with a hastily organized force, stopped the British attack upon New Orleans. In the struggle at the Chalmette battle site, even though heavily outnumbered, and with the British forces having far superior firepower, the

scrappy Americans handily won the famous battle. During the battle the British used rockets as a scare tactic for the first time in Louisiana, in hopes of bewildering the rag-tag troops. It apparently not

only did not affect the aim of the American riflemen and cannoneers, but it inspired the further use of fireworks, including rockets, after the great victory. For several years, New Orleans celebrated the day when "the people of Louisiana first showed that they were willing to seal with their blood the compact that had already indissolubly bound them to the great American public", as the Louisiana Gazette newspaper said on December 23, 1816. A circus that year put on a "grand display of fireworks" in honor of the anniversary, L-Ami des Lois reported on December 23, 1816. Since then the victory has been celebrated each year on January 8th, when the last phase of the Battle of New Orleans and the War of 1812 was fought.

New Orleans had a population of only 8,000 when the

tradition started. The city grew rapidly and, with it, so did the general enthusiasm for fireworks. As soon as the merchants could stock up, the people took the celebration into their own hands, not willing for the political authorities to have a monopoly on patriotic expression.

By 1860, the population reached 168,000. The enthusiasm for fireworks grew, along with the "explosion of crackers, fireworks and firearms". The celebration became so loud the Daily Picayune reported that one man was actually driven crazy.

Two years later, during the Civil War, when New Orleans had fallen to Union arms, the Daily Delta on December 24, 1862, commented on the "popping" of firecrackers and asked "what would the rising generation do without them?" By then, Christmas and New Year's Eve had assimilated the fireworks tradition. By the end of the century, when the city had grown to 287,000, fireworks were heard and seen beginning in mid December and soaring to the double climax of Christmas Eve and New Year's Eve.

During these times, the sight was unbelievable. At night the sky glowed with Roman candles and rocket bursts; hot air balloons of tissue paper trailing alcohol flames carried the danger of fire far and wide. Buying gun powder in grocery stores, boys set off toy cannons, which cost 10-25¢, and devised other explosions.

As early as 1807, the city government of New Orleans penalized the use of fireworks, except by authorized persons, by a fine of $5-$10. This did absolutely no good, nor did the ordinance of 1817, as the Argus stated on December 28, 1826; nor did the enactment of a new law that year, raising the fine to $50. Other laws in subsequent years proved equally ineffective.

In more-recent years, because of the nightly use of fireworks for six months during the 1984 World's Fair, and with

1984 WORLD'S FAIR

the more-frequent use of fireworks displays in the open area along the river front by Woldenberg Park, it seems fireworks are more popular now than ever before.

A new wrinkle to an old tradition is the use of indoor fireworks for concerts, Mardi Gras celebrations, conventions, etc. In 1991, during a Monday night NFL football game which was broadcast nationwide, a fireworks display in the Superdome led to a minor fire at the ceiling of the dome, requiring a brave maintenance man to climb the rafters with an extinguisher to put the fire out while a Saints game was in progress on the field. That particular fireworks display and aftermath were seen all over the United States. It was also nationally televised by all the networks on their news shows.

One could say this was just another way of our letting the rest of the country know that New Orleans is truly a hot place to visit.

In spite of New Orleans having ordinances for 188 years forbidding the use of firecrackers, the city is no closer to curbing the use of fireworks today than it was in 1807.

CHAPTER FIVE

LAGNIAPPE

INTRODUCTION

The following, you will find, is not historical, pictorial or triviatorial. For the lack of a better description, it is listed as "Lagniappe". It simply means to receive not only full value but a little extra when making a purchase.

The material begins with a tribute to the two men I looked upon as father figures. As you will learn upon reading, both lived long lives and died within a very short time of each other. They also left indelible imprints on those with whom they came in contact. Since previous books I authored had only a short dedication to them, I kindly request your indulging me by allowing me to pay extended tribute to them in this book.

I am confident that after reading of their simple, family-oriented lives, they will serve as much of an inspiration to you as they did for me and others who knew them. The chapter ends with a memorable toast I learned from a gentleman in his nineties.

A TRIBUTE TO THE IRON MAN
ABNER J. STALL
December 17, 1896 - January 3, 1995

He was called Ab by his loving wife Theresa, Uncle Ab by relatives, and Grandpa by his grandchildren. By the masses who knew him, he was always referred to as the "Iron Man". The term Iron Man came about when he was a professional fighter. He was known to have hands of iron, a body to match, and a will to win that never left him. The Iron Man title stuck, and was reinforced when he became a machinist. In all of his working days, he never had just one job. He

Iron Man' ready for action

always held two and sometimes three different jobs simultaneously. His quest for work was generated by need, not greed. His first son, Abner, was asthmatic and for many, many years required great medical assistance. He was a proud man who took great pride in providing for his family without need of outside assistance.

The Iron Man was a real survivor. He survived the Great Depression. Once, he jokingly said things were so bad during the Great Depression, that some of his friends got married just to get the rice. He found humor everywhere. He no doubt used it as a survival technique. He also survived the greatest of all curses, the curse of the devil, as he labeled it. By that, he meant he buried his first-born son, whom he had proudly given his name. This tragedy, two years later, was compounded by the death of his life-long partner and wife, to whom he was married for 72 years.

The Iron Man was also a dreamer. Just before he expired, he was in the process of making plans for his 100th birthday party, which he said would be a real doozy. It would, as always, be a sit-down dinner, where his family and friends would be comfortable. He wanted to have internationally renowned Pete Fountain play for this special occasion. When asked how he might get Pete, he said when he belonged to the Golden Agers, he knew Pete's Mama and said that she was one hell of a good dancer. He would simply get her to speak to Pete on his behalf. Being a dutiful son, Pete would say "Yes" just as Jesus said yes to Mary when she requested more wine for the wedding feast.

The old boy even knew what songs he wanted Pete to play. After dinner, he said the music would start off with "It's So Nice To Have A Man Around The House" -- that he sang to his wife on many occasions, followed by "Won't You Come Home, Bill Bailey, Won't You Come Home", Theresa's favorite song. The evening would end with "A Closer Walk With Thee" for nobody plays it like Pete. His dream was to dance at his 100th birthday party with every female who attended, for he felt like Fred Astaire when he was on the dance floor.

To those who were fortunate to know him, Iron Man

was a living example of the old saying, "It is better to give than to receive." He never wanted anything for himself. He wore Thom McAn, not Bally shoes from Switzerland. He wore lots of khaki and blue jeans, never owned a Botany 500 suit from New York. He didn't drink champagne from France, but delighted in a cold draft -- O'Doul's non-alcoholic beer towards the end. He drove a plain old Ford, and never had the desire for a Lincoln Continental. Because of his deep desire to share what he had with others, he had what many with more capital never had. He felt the most important thing was love of his family and respect of everyone that came in contact with him. It has been said that if he met a stranger who was down and out and needed $2 and he had only $1 in his pocket, he would go out and borrow or work for the other dollar to see to it that the person in need had exactly what he needed, never less.

Ninety eight years is a long time to live. Being a laboring man all his life with much of his work being done outdoors, his body was greatly weathered. This was compounded by his stays in the hospital in the latter years, where they probed and stuck and blackened his skin. Though his body was weathered and tattered, his face on the day he died, had no wrinkles, and the skin was as smooth and soft as a baby's bottom. The reason for that phenomenon no doubt lies in the fact his face was a true reflection of his soul. It, too, was pure and always wore a smile that was infectious. He could say more with that twinkle in his eyes and a smile that seemed to be frozen on his face than any great orator could ever expound in words.

As a true Christian, he lived what Jesus taught. He was a symbol of love and charity through his desire to help his fellow man. He was a man who worked hard and played equally as hard, time permitting. His simple philosophy was to never speak ill of anyone, even if they deserved the criticism. He simply would say nothing if he had nothing good to say.

He was a man who was punctual to a fault, never being late for any event in his lifetime. He never made a visit to a person's home without carrying a loaf of bread, a bag of fruit, a container of raw oysters, or something else good to eat to share with his friends.

Iron Man, you have now reached your greatest reward. As a true Christian, you believed life on earth followed by death leads to eternal life in Heaven with God, your mother and father, your wife Theresa, son Abner, your sister Elsa, and brother John. You may be gone, but you will always live in the fond memories of all that you helped while here on earth.

In closing, each time we see someone do a good deed by helping someone in need, the next time we eat a piece of raw garlic, turkey stuffed with oyster dressing, gumbo without rice, cabbage and ham hocks, and drink the pot liquor from the bottom of the plate, or drink a cold brew, we will all be thinking of you.

Since you so graciously helped us all here on earth, I can picture you in Heaven putting in a good word every day to God on our behalf. As a machinist almost all of your life, I can see you putting ball-bearing hinges on the gates of Heaven making sure they are properly oiled, and at the same time bringing a bag of fruit, a loaf of fresh bread and a container of oysters to St. Peter, so when we ultimately get there, he will be in a good mood.

May God bless you, Iron Man, for you were truly a blessing to all of us while here on earth.

TRIBUTE TO
WILLIAM C. STALL
July 31, 1901 - March 11, 1995

Per or Uncle Bill, that's what most of us called him, and we did so with great affection and respect.

I know that most of the family called him "Per", but to me he was always Uncle Bill. I looked upon him as my second father. The reason for that feeling, Uncle Bill and my father, "The Iron Man", were brothers, and his wife, Aunt Lena, and my mother, Theresa, were sisters. With two brothers marrying two sisters, you can imagine we were very close.

I feel that our two families were probably closer than any two families I have ever known, although I could be partial in that area.

For many years, we celebrated all holidays as one family sitting at one big table specifically built for that purpose. For Christmas, Thanksgiving and all major holidays, we were never separated. Separation did not happen until we, the children, all married and went our separate ways.

Every summer, when my family lived in Covington, Louisiana, because of my brother's health, my cousins, Jake, Steve, Billy and Paul spent almost the entire summer with my family in Covington. It was there, with the help of Uncle Bill, we all learned to swim in the mighty Tchefuncta River. His teaching method, although a little unorthodox, did work. He took us in a boat into deep water where he threw us in and told us to follow him. It was a good thing he taught us to swim at an early age. My Aunt Lena could float like a log, but never learned to swim. She was so relaxed when floating, she would actually fall asleep and would often drift out into deep water. Uncle Bill told us little kids our job was to bring Aunt Lena back to shallow water without waking her up. Most of the time, she didn't even know the danger she was in.

When we all got together on weekends, we were one big mass of people. Every part of the comfortable, old, squeaky house was slept in. Not only did Uncle Bill and Aunt Lena come and join us for weekends, but many of our other relatives did so likewise. Swimming on those weekends became our only way of bathing, for the bathtub was always iced down and filled with watermelons. On one particular weekend, a misfortune occurred that became our good fortune. A truck on the edge of town, carrying thousands of chickens, turned over. Word got out that the chickens running loose were fair game. Uncle Bill put all of us kids in the old Model T truck and drove us to the area. We rounded up scores of chickens and brought them home; we had one heck of a good feast that particular weekend and many weekends to follow. We had far more chickens than even our large group could consume. The chickens laid eggs and reproduced and furnished us with stewed chicken and eggs for a long, long time. While speaking of food, Uncle Bill, it was said, could and did eat anything that did not eat him. His stomach, it appeared, was made of cast iron, just like his cast iron belief in right, fairness and compassion.

For spending money as children, Uncle Bill suggested we catch frogs. When he would come for the weekend, he would take them back to the florist in New Orleans and sell them for a penny apiece. Nothing was too much trouble for Uncle Bill when it came to his family. It was he who taught me that little things don't mean a lot; they mean everything. To this day, that quote is framed and on the wall of my office, and each employee that comes to work receives a copy of that plaque as a reminder of what is expected of him or her.

As kids coming up during, and right after the depression, we may not have had many material things, but we had the most important things there are on earth, including the deep love and affection that was shown to us by Uncle Bill and others. He was truly one of those unique people who not only believed, but practiced, that old adage - it is better to give than receive.

I personally feel that I was doubly blessed with having two fathers, for I, through the examples of Uncle Bill and "The Iron Man", learned much as a child even though I didn't know it at the time.

As a youngster, I served as helper when Uncle Bill did plumbing work and other handyman jobs for his own home and all of his neighbors. He did not charge them for what he did, for they were his neighbors. To this day, I feel my work ethics were molded by Uncle Bill. He taught me much, and I repeat, not by preaching but through his example.

When my wife, Margaret, and I married, our dream, like

many other young couples, was to some day own our own home. Uncle Bill encouraged and assisted us in buying a lot to help us get started. I remember that the big lot we wanted was more than we could afford, so Uncle Bill offered to buy half of the lot, which he really didn't need, just so that we could have what we wanted. He did it as an act of kindness, I'm sure, without realizing it.

That's the kind of man Uncle Bill was. Whenever we needed advice, we were always comfortable asking Uncle Bill for his guidance, and he was always there for us. Not very long ago, my wife and I expressed our deep appreciation for what he did for us. He said he really didn't remember anything special that he did.

Whenever people think of great men, they often think of people like Einstein, Dr. DeBakey and General Schwartzkopf. I hope that when you think of a great man, you will think of my Uncle Bill, as I do.

In my humble estimation, he was, and others like him are, truly what make up the backbone of this great country. Uncle Bill had a simple formula for life that I have gladly followed. It is, simply desire, dedication and determination, coupled with persistence and the proper attitude.

Uncle Bill's number one priority all of his life was his family, not becoming the wealthiest man in the city. In the end, I know he was the richest man in the city, for he had what money could not buy. He earned the love and respect of all who knew him. As I mingled with those who attended his wake, almost to a person they related stories of what he did for them. One lady shared the fact that he drove her to the hospital when she had her baby, who is now 50 years old. She said there was nothing he could ask that she would not gladly do. "But, you know Uncle Bill", she said, "he would never ask for anything; his joy came in giving."

His lack of a higher education did not hamper him from being an inspiration to all who came in contact with him, again through his teaching by example. He had no degree in philosophy or engineering; his degree was the one most difficult to achieve; it was the degree of hard knocks.

You may not have learned much about him through the electronic or print media. Where he did make it into print was in the most important place, the book of good deeds kept in heaven.

Charity is defined as giving without expecting anything in return. Chances are, and I am not a betting man, this, too, I learned from Uncle Bill, but if I were I would bet Uncle Bill touched the lives of almost everyone here today in one way or another, and he did it in the true meaning of charity. In closing, Uncle Bill, I ask everyone here today to join me in a toast to you. It may seem out of place in a chapel, but I feel sure God would gladly give us His blessing. Several years ago, I heard a 95-year-old man give this toast, and I shall never forget it, just as I hope you will never forget Uncle Bill. If this toast was not written for Uncle Bill, it should have been. I kindly ask that you raise your hand.

May I wish each and every one of you every day of your lives to steal, swear and lie. Yes, I did say to steal, swear and lie. Steal a little time everyday to help those less fortunate than yourself.

Swear to do only those things that are right in the eyes of the Lord. And be sure to lie in the arms of the one you love every night and tell them that you love them.

Uncle Bill, we will always love you, and I assure you you will not be forgotten, for you will live within us for the rest of our lives.

MEMORABLE TOAST

As a fitting end, I would like to offer a toast I heard several years ago when I had the pleasure of serving as master of ceremonies for a foster grandparents annual awards banquet. There were several hundred lovely ladies and gentlemen, all 65 and older, in attendance. A 90-year-old gentleman was the recipient of the top award. After he received and graciously accepted the beautiful plaque, he started to go back to his table. Several people shouted from the audience, "Make him give his toast." As master of ceremonies, I replied by stating that it would not be appropriate to make him give the toast, but we would all be honored if he would share the toast with us. He graciously agreed. He asked all to please lift their glasses. Once they did, he said, "May I wish each and every one of you every day of your lives steal, swear and lie." With that, people looked at each other befuddled. After the crowd settled down, he continued. "Yes," he said, "steal a little time every day to help those less fortunate. Swear to do only those things in the eyes of the Lord and be sure to lie in the arms of the one you love every night and tell them that you love them."

I loved writing and sharing the colorful history of the Crescent City. I only hope you enjoyed reading it half as much as I enjoyed doing the research and writing.

GREAT BUDDY STALL BOOKS NOW AVAILABLE
1. Buddy Stall's Big Easy
2. Buddy Stall's French Quarter Montage
3. Buddy Stall's Sometimes We Must Laugh To Keep From Crying
4. Proud, Peculiar New Orleans: The Inside Story
5. Buddy Stall's Louisiana Potpourri
6. Buddy Stall's New Orleans
7. Mardi Gras and Bacchus, Something Old and Something New
8. Buddy Stall's Crescent City

ART CREDITS:
Photography and Drawings

References are to page numbers.

Lane Casteix: 9, 10, 14, 23, 31, 35, 40, 41, 50, 55, 57, 59, 60, 61, 70, 74, 77, 84, 88, 91, 96, 99, 100, 101, 103, 127, 128, 131, 132, 134, 135, 136, 139, 142, 143, 146, 147, 148, 153, 154, 155, 156, 157, 158, 160, 161, 162, 163, 164, 165, 168, 169, 171, 173, 175, 177, 178, 179, 180, 181, 182, 183, 184, 186, 187, 188, 189, 191, 192, 198, 199, 200, 201, 202, 204, 208, 209, 210, 219, 221, 222, 225, 226, 227, 229, 230, 231, 232, 233, 234, 235, 236, 238, 239, 244, 245, 246, 247

Buddy Stall: 19, 25, 27, 30, 34, 36, 46, 47, 48, 58, 68, 69, 71, 73, 75, 76, 79, 82, 85, 89, 91, 92, 104, 107, 108, 112, 113, 114, 118, 119, 120, 122, 123, 124, 125, 126, 127, 128, 133, 137, 138, 140, 141, 143, 144, 145, 147, 148, 149, 150, 152, 154, 159, 160, 161, 166, 167, 168, 170, 172, 173, 176, 178, 179, 185, 192, 193, 201, 225, 252, 256

Jules Cahn: 11, 12

Henri Gandolfo: 12

Roy Cappel: 15, 16

Longue Vue Gardens: 20, 21, 22

Charles Frank: 26

Arthur Schott: 39, 42

Wemco: 52

Robert Timphony: 80

Martin Marietta: 81

Stella Sagona Reynolds: 87

Clyde Morrison: 94

City of New Orleans: 118

Bill Cresson: 140

Phil Johnson: 141

Roy Todd: 167

Al Whiteman: 190